MW01633143

Right from the beginning this book invites you into the kind of soul posture we all need daily. That in the midst of the pressure and noise and stress and tasks of life, taking a few minutes with Jesus through the Scriptures he gave us, to focus, calm, get our hearts and heads right before taking on the day. These are more the 60 'devotionals'; they are 60 deep and practical reflections on some of the best and most powerful passages in the whole Bible, framed in a way that gets us to focus on the most important thing so that we get the most out of life. As the cover suggests. If life is at times a storm, cold, windy, tumultuous, time with Jesus in the Scriptures, even for these 60 days, is a roof over our head, a warm fire to keep us alive in the face of the chill of life, and the comfort of a good meal to sustain us when it feels there is little hope we will ever feel safe again. Victor has brought us into that house, and sat us at the feet of Jesus in a way we all need. Thank you my friend, you have a gift, and I will treasure this book for years to come.

- Mark Clark, Teaching Pastor of Bayside Church

"In Him All Things" is like sitting down with a good friend who calls you to live your best life on the mission with Jesus. It's raw, real, and full of insights that will challenge and encourage you every day. If you're ready to dive deeper and find real peace in the middle of life's craziness, this is the book for you.

- Wes Davis, Lead Pastor of New Life Church

"Like many daily devotionals, In Him All Things focuses on a different piece of scripture each day. But rather than simply offering affirmations or comfort, Victor approaches each passage like the person he is, a pastor who deeply cares for the discipleship of his flock. Each day offers insightful context and interpretation of the text, empathy and understanding for our shared human condition and Western experience, and challenges the reader to move forward with intentionality into a deepening practice of faith."

- Ruth McGillivray, Executive Vice-President
Northwest Seminary & College

IN HIM ALL THINGS

IN HIM ALL THINGS

A SIXTY DAY DEVOTIONAL

VICTOR MAYNARD

ISBN: 978-1-0690218

First Edition

To my beautiful and brilliant wife Kristen, to think it all started with some late night nachos.

For in him all things were created:
things in heaven and on earth,
visible and invisible,
whether thrones or powers or rulers or authorities;
all things have been created
through him and for him.
He is before all things,
and in him all things hold together.

COLOSSIANS 1:16-17

CONTENTS

FOREWORD

You are not an accident. No matter how you were conceived. I am not an accident. Neither is any other person you and I know. Someone wants you to exist. Someone wants me to exist. Someone wants you and me to be alive. In particular to be alive in relationship with Him.

That Someone is, of course, the Living God. The God Who has revealed Himself to be Father, Son and Holy Spirit. A relational God. Who has lived for all eternity as relationship in relationship. Who spoke us into being in order to enjoy the Divine relationality. To not only live with Him but in Him.

In.

The gospel is in that little word, in that little preposition.

In.

The heart of Jesus' call upon our lives. "Abide in Me and I in you" (John 15:15). In. It seems to be our number one task, or job, in life. "Make your home in Me, and I will make My home in you." Or as the apostle Paul put it in his dialogue with the philosophers in Athens, quoting one of his contemporary thinkers, "In Him we live and move and have our being" (Acts 17:28). In. And as Paul puts it in the early Christian hymn in his letter to the believers in Colossae, "in Him all things hold together" (1:15). All things! In. The great missionary of the 20th century, E. Stanley Jones, often said, "You cannot get closer than in." In.

Victor Maynard is one of the finest young pastoral theologians I know. That is what a pastor is, a pastoral theologian. Whenever I am with him, I am taken by his gentleness, his kindness, his thoughtfulness, his rootedness, all born of his yearning to know God in Jesus. And I am taken by his honesty. Honesty about the challenges in seeking to live out what he knows God in Jesus is offering us.

In the book you are holding in your hands, Victor takes us into sixty passages of the Bible that from different perspectives speak of the wonder of in. You will see that he does help us reflect on the passages, but then moves us to reflect on how our hearts and minds are responding to what the Holy Spirit is saying in the passage, especially how we might be afraid of what we hear, or resist what we hear, or how we long to live what we hear.

Victor's desire in what he has written is that we grow more deeply aware of and rejoicing more fully in the wonder of being called to live in.

We are not accidents of some impersonal process. Someone wants us to be alive. Alive in His very life.

INTRODUCTION

All things have been created through Jesus and for Jesus.

When we open our Bibles and allow his words to rest in our soul, we should once again recognize that our life, like all things, is found in him. Yet, now and again, that is not our experience. The daily ritual of engaging with scripture doesn't always provide a sense of spiritual closeness. It is a book that is holy, vibrant, and perfect; but, at times, it is also strange and unfamiliar. To find life in this ancient book is not always an easy task, especially when it doesn't have our full and earnest attention. The prerequisite for seeing God in his words is clear: "You will seek me and find me when you seek me with all your heart." (Jer. 29:13). All of our heart. That means He wants more than a mind already preoccupied with the day's errands. He wants more than a heart solely seeking emotionally satisfying answers in the text. God wants all of us when we sit before his words. It is only fitting, since Colossians 1:16 states, "All things [including our feeble hearts] are for him".

In all honesty, this presents a vision that's a bit rigorous and exhausting. Even though Jesus is entitled to our undivided attention and unhurried presence, it can often feel like another demanding expectation on an already busy life. Why, though, do we lump reading the Bible in with cleaning the house, preparing a work presentation, or making lunches for the kids in the morning? Viewing scripture reading as simply another chore to cross off the list is far from compelling. And it's definitely not what Jesus wants from us.

Jesus calls us to seek him with everything we've got because he doesn't want us to miss out on the life he has available. If we're walking through the woods on a stormy night and we know there is a warm and dry house nearby, we'll do whatever we can to seek it out. When we see glimpses of light through the trees, we move quickly towards shelter. Outside the door, we feel the warmth of the fire and hear Jesus call to us, "All of you!" He wants our heart, mind, desires, fears, and hopes to enter the house. Despite having every right to command us in, Jesus offers it as an invitation.

To engage with God's word isn't another daily task, but rather an invitation to come in from the cold. We give all of ourselves to find life in these words because we want our whole selves to be warmed by the fire – our intellects stimulated, hearts understood, desires met, fears dissolved, and, ultimately, souls satisfied in the House of the Lord. You are created to be there. You are created for Jesus.

As you read each of these devotionals, pray for something that is impossible in your own strength. Pray that you would give Jesus all of yourself as you read, reflect, and find Him.

I am the good shepherd. The good shepherd lays down his life for the sheep. The hired hand is not the shepherd and does not own the sheep. So when he sees the wolf coming, he abandons the sheep and runs away. Then the wolf attacks the flock and scatters it.

JOHN 10:11-13

JESUS IS OUR GOOD SHEPHERD. The word "good" (kalos) is often used in scripture to mean surpassing or better. By calling himself our good shepherd, Jesus acknowledges he is not the only shepherd available. There are other guides in the wilderness on offer for our souls. Jesus is well aware that we are pulled by these different voices (Isaiah 53:6), especially our own. But he invites us into something better. Here we find the crux of our own discipleship: in this very moment, as Jesus once again calls us to him, do you believe he is better?

Remember, the Judean deserts were some seriously rough places. Food and water were scarce, dangers abounded, and sheep had little chance of making it far alone. Having a shepherd was not merely a comfort - it was a necessity. Likewise, it is a necessity for us in our modern-day desert. As we navigate the rough terrain of moral chaos and an ethical wilderness on our own, it is easy to get thrashed around. Unwise choices, toxic relationships, and harmful ideologies leave us scattered. The Good Shepherd offers to lead us on a different path.

Here is the kicker: we struggle to take it.

I often feel the pull to carve out my own path in the barren desert – perhaps you do too. So many of us would rather embrace pain, move past unresolved guilt, or bury anxieties to prove to the world we can do it on our own. But to make this the mantra of our lives will cost us greatly. Every morning, the Good Shepherd graciously calls us to place our obsessive need for control at his feet and to follow him. Alternate guides may equally promise goodness, but Jesus is the only one who can back it up with a radical act of laying down his life for his sheep.

So, here is where we are left: when feeling the pull to stray into the desert alone today, will you trust the Good Shepherd and everything he has on offer for you?

Then they entrusted it to the men appointed to supervise the work on the Lord's temple. These men paid the workers who repaired and restored the temple. They also gave money to the carpenters and builders to purchase dressed stone, and timber for joists and beams for the buildings that the kings of Judah had allowed to fall into ruin. The workers labored faithfully... While they were bringing out the money that had been taken into the temple of the Lord, Hilkiah the priest found the Book of the Law of the Lord that had been given through Moses.

2 CHRONICLES 34:10-12, 14

AS A KING WHO RULED IN JERUSALEM, Josiah certainly left his mark. Leading one of the biggest spiritual reformations in the nation's history, he smashes the idols of false gods into powder and spreads their remains over the graves of leaders who worshiped them (2 Chron. 34:4). It's a bit dramatic, sure. The message, however, is delivered: Israel is out of the idol worship business, and Yahweh will be put in his rightful place. As Josiah continues to clean up the nation and rebuild the temple, a dusty old relic is discovered. This relic just so happens to be the Mosaic Law. It's a game changer that sets Israel on a trajectory of repentance and renewal.

The words of life were buried under God's neglected and ruined temple. And who does God use to unearth his forgotten law? The finest craftsmen. By skillfully shaping precious stones and timber, these men begin to rebuild what was left common and forgotten into something revered and sacred. The passage says they "labored faithfully." In return, God faithfully brings an entire community back to life. Renewal doesn't happen through priestly hands with incense and scepters, but through weathered hands with chisel and hammer.

We often confine God's work to pietistic practices: actions that seem monastic and mystical. Our love to paint, fix cars, grow fresh produce, or program software somehow belongs in a different category, as if it's irrelevant to God's redemptive plan. Yet, in this story, God takes note of faithful carpenters, and he stitches their efforts perfectly into his plan. 1 Corinthians 10:31 states, "So whether you eat or drink or whatever you do, do it all for the glory of God." Managing your sales team, disciplining your teenager, or changing light bulbs for your grandparents all have the opportunity to glorify God. Spiritual significance becomes infused into what might feel mundane or repetitive. Anyone can choose to faithfully glorify God. The question is: what is in your hands? Whether they are filled with paperwork, garden soil or a nursing baby, do it faithfully to the glory of God.

> One day at about three in the afternoon he had a vision. He distinctly saw an angel of God, who came to him and said, "Cornelius!" Cornelius stared at him in fear. "What is it, Lord?" he asked. The angel answered, "Your prayers and gifts to the poor have come up as a memorial offering before God.
>
> *ACTS 10:3-4*

GOD MEETS PEOPLE in the most unexpected places. Cornelius lived in the heart of Caesarea. This city was built as a monument to Caesar and the Roman way of life. In many respects, its very construction is the antithesis of God's kingdom. The Jews hated the city so much they called it "the daughter of Esau."[1] Yet, it is here God turns his ear to a Centurion's prayers. In this unexpected space, God graciously draws his attention to a "God-fearer" consistent in prayer and generosity. In a city constructed as a tribute to man's ambition, the angel reassures Cornelius his prayers have constructed a different type of tribute.

We don't often think about prayer this way. Prayer seems abstract and unquantifiable; it is probably a reason we aren't always drawn to it. What does it accomplish? How can I know? Is God even listening? In this passage, we notice two things. First, we find a place and a people spurned by the Jews, but not by God. Unconcerned with position, upbringing, culture, language, or location, God is constantly doing reconnaissance across the earth, looking for those whose hearts are towards him (2 Chron.16:9). In many ways, Cornelius is a product of Roman culture; however, by looking beyond the impressive medals and decorative armor, God finds a humble heart pointed toward him, and that is enough. That simple qualifier remains today. God leans into the words of a contrite heart (Ps. 51:17). We know he resists the proud, but he also pulls up a chair for those who recognize their complete need for him.

Second, we hear the angel use concrete language for what feels like an abstract concept. Prayer is the brick-and-mortar of a tribute placed before God, as if each prayer has a compounding effect upon another. We often measure the worth of a prayer by whether or not it is answered; it seems, however, God places value on the practice of faithfully praying itself. The constant appeal to heaven is not only noticed, but honored – regardless of the outcome.

Prayer isn't transactional. It's not about getting results. It is a familiar place to rendezvous with God. And choosing to continually show up in that space matters to God. It is an offering to Him. Even when we feel our words are falling flat, if our hearts are positioned correctly, God catches each word we utter. It is in these very moments that a tribute is being built.

> Come to me, all you who are weary and burdened, and I will give you rest. Take my yoke upon you and learn from me, for I am gentle and humble in heart, and you will find rest for your souls. For my yoke is easy and my burden is light."
>
> *MATTHEW 11:28-30*

WHAT A BEAUTIFUL INVITATION. Jesus bids us to himself not based on what we have accomplished, who we know, or the position in which we find ourselves. On the contrary, he calls on those who are exhausted and at the end of themselves. At first glance, this passage seems to provide a sense of comfort from the burdens the world presses down on us. But is this what Jesus is really getting at? In its original language, Greek has three different voices: passive, middle, and active. The word "burdened" (phortizō) is written in the middle voice, implying an action done to self. In short, these are self-inflicted wounds.[2] These are burdens that come wrapped in promises of freedom, control, pleasure, and comfort; instead, they have become yokes that drag us through the muddy fields of life.

Jesus' offer of a yoke is only bizarre to those convinced they aren't wearing one in the first place. In reality, we are all affected by our various environments. These environments pitch a particular vision of the good life and have us chart a course toward it with our whole being. No one is exempt. Career ambition, sexual liberty, and religious piety are obvious vehicles that drive us toward our life's vision, but they usually leave us rolled over in the ditch. Even those of us who think we walk through life with eyes wide open miss the more subtle yokes we throw on each morning. Baking your famous cookies for the office seems like an act of Christian hospitality, but it can be driven by a profound need to be liked and accepted. Filling your teenager's calendar with extracurricular activities feels like a sacrificial investment, but perhaps it is rooted in an anxious need for parental control. Heavy yokes can be cloaked in noble acts, and Jesus is convinced they will run us thin.

What does Jesus' yoke offer us? Rest. He fashions a yoke that helps us learn how to be in perfect pace with him. Not frantically rushing ahead or aimlessly slugging behind, but in step with our Savior. It is no coincidence that this sits on the backdrop of the Sermon on the Mount. Jesus' way of life liberates us from the burdensome yokes that demand more from us than they deliver.

I imagine you're tired – the type of tiredness that a good sleep or Netflix binge can't quite remedy. There is a tiredness that comes from slipping out of Jesus' easy yoke and carrying loads we aren't built for. It is important to ask the hard questions to draw some light on your condition. What am I most stressed about? What do I think about before I fall asleep? Am I hopeful about the future? Have I been a present listener lately? A scattered soul is a tired soul, and as you read this, know that Jesus' invitation is for you at this very moment.

> Then a teacher of the law came to him and said, "Teacher, I will follow you wherever you go." Jesus replied, "Foxes have dens and birds have nests, but the Son of Man has no place to lay his head."
>
> *MATTHEW 8:19-20*

HERE WE HAVE A SCRIBE who has done his research and is convinced. He boldly proclaims to Jesus he is in for the ride, no matter where it takes him. This would be a dream for most pastors. You take the guy at his word and sort out the rest later. Jesus, however, does the opposite. Where we ease people into discipleship slowly and comfortably, Jesus front-loads it. His next line confronts the scribe's biggest hang-up: comfort. He warns him the journey involves uprooting his biggest attachments to this world. One where the usual comforts are left at home. In a very real way, Jesus demands everything of this man's life in one response.

Jesus was renowned for this. He always drew lines between admirer and disciple. Soren Kierkegaard expands on this: "The admirer never makes any true sacrifices. He always plays it safe. Though in words, phrases, songs, he is inexhaustible about how highly he prizes Christ, [yet] he renounces nothing".[3] Have you ever experienced that? It feels like Jesus is burning the bridge behind you. There is no option to just stay here or go back. To be a disciple is to move forward into deeper consecration, trust, and surrender to Jesus. These sacred moments happen more often than we would probably prefer. Jesus is kind enough to continually trim off our attachments to the world. Many of us probably resonate with the scribe's attachment to comfort.

Here is why it matters. To find comfort and security in anything other than Jesus means we must protect it at any cost. If it's found in our home, we pour more resources into extending square footage and building pools. If it's in our work, we step on teammates and compete to secure our position. If it's in our relationships, we compromise ourselves to fit the mold of others. And you begin to become an island unto yourself – one that gets smaller and smaller as it becomes more rigid and immovable. The world you build must be protected. Yet, Jesus calls all of us out into the waters (Matthew 14:29). He calls us to him. The invitation is to not plant your stake in a bigger house that will be rubble in a few decades, but in the one who is "a fortified tower; [where] the righteous run to it and are safe" (Proverbs 18:10). He is our comfort.

This is going to look different for everyone. We don't all need to sell our houses or quit our jobs, but we do need to take an honest look at our lives and examine what we have taken off the table for Jesus to change, remove, or restore. When he calls us from an admirer to a disciple, do we trust him with every part of our lives?

When John, who was in prison, heard about the deeds of the Messiah, he sent his disciples to ask him, "Are you the one who is to come, or should we expect someone else?" Jesus replied, "Go back and report to John what you hear and see: The blind receive sight, the lame walk, those who have leprosy are cleansed, the deaf hear, the dead are raised, and the good news is proclaimed to the poor. Blessed is anyone who does not stumble on account of me."

MATTHEW 11:2-6

JOHN THE BAPTIST has a really strong start. He comes out of the wilderness bright-eyed and ready to shake things up. He doesn't hold back any punches, preaching the kingdom, calling people to repentance, and baptizing those who believed. And with that kind of message, as you can imagine, a following formed around him. At the peak of his ministry, Jesus presents himself and calls John to baptize him. For John, this is it. It is clear the Messiah has come and the whole redemptive story is coming together. Most scholars believe when John throws around end-time judgments in the preceding verses, he is convinced this is all going down in his lifetime (Matt. 3:10-12). Surely, Jesus is here to set up his throne and judge the world.

Fast-forward a few chapters: John's ministry lands him in jail. With only his thoughts to keep him company, he forms a question: "Are you the one who is to come, or should we expect someone else?" (Matt. 11:3) He does the math, and his vision of the Messiah isn't quite adding up. There are moments when our expectations of Jesus need a course correction. Depending on how drastic the correction, it can leave us disheartened and questioning core tenants of our faith. That can be a dangerous place to stay. In Exodus 6, Pharoah doubles the labor for the Hebrew slaves, leaving them spiraling in despair. They are so disheartened they are unable to hear the promise of rescue through Moses (Ex.6:9). Jesus refuses to leave John brooding for too long. He injects hope and faith in John's heart with report after report of Jesus' kingdom making serious ground on earth (v.4-5).

There is nothing wrong with doubting the journey as you traverse tough terrain, but remember you have a guide. Jesus is well aware of our unsettling doubts. All he asks is to be invited into the conversation. He is abundantly patient with our process. His compassion becomes evident as the chapter unfolds. Jesus never critiques or rebukes John for asking the question; in fact, he celebrates his faith to his disciples.

The wicked flee though no one pursues,
but the righteous are as bold as a lion.

JOHN 10:11-13

THERE IS A FLOODED MARKET for one particular product: self-confidence. Everywhere we look, we bump into articles, books, or podcasts offering the best path towards boosting your confidence. It is presented as the silver bullet for interviews, first dates, promotions, or simply being the best version of yourself. It is rocket fuel for reaching your potential. This, however, is not a passage about self-confidence.

Self-confidence is a learned tactic – one used to position yourself more favorably in a transactional society. Boldness, on the other hand, isn't mustered from within: it is a gift from the Spirit for the good of others. Look at Peter. Not long ago, Jesus is dragged into the courtroom of the High Priest Annas to be unjustly accused. What does Peter do? He hovers around the perimeter until caught, and then denies knowing Jesus. Crippled by fear, he saves his own neck and flees. In Acts 4, Peter steps back into the house of his greatest failure. After preaching the gospel, he is dragged into the same courtroom, in front of the same High Priest, knowing it could lead to the same outcome. Something is different this time, however. He is "filled with the Holy Spirit" (Acts 4:8). Peter receives what he could never learn from any article. He receives boldness from the Holy Spirit. Instead of shrinking back, he steps toward the powers of the day and preaches unhindered. And what is the response?

"When they saw the courage of Peter and John and realized that they were unschooled, ordinary men, they were astonished and they took note that these men had been with Jesus." They have seen this type of courage before. Remembering how Jesus responded to his accusers, torturers, and executioners, they know, "these men had been with Jesus."

There is no power in masking our fears with inflated self-confidence. When the Holy Spirit fills you, he ministers to your most prevalent fears by giving you the grace to boldly step out in spite of them. That is a courage people notice. A courage that makes a difference. When was the last time you asked for boldness? Take some time to examine where you have perhaps shrunk back. You may be reluctant to confess something to a friend, stand on a conviction at work, or simply share the good news to a neighbor. Ask the Holy Spirit to fill you.

I lift up my eyes to the mountains
where does my help come from?
My help comes from the Lord,
the Maker of heaven and earth.

PSALMS 121:1-2

WHERE DO YOU FIND HOPE? Many of us have a defining moment in our lives where we look upon the object of our hope and realize it doesn't quite deliver. When this happens, you either cut ties completely or lean in harder. There is a strong temptation to ring out your idol for all its worth to just get a couple drops of satisfaction. The Psalmist "lifts his eyes to the mountains." Why? In those days, mountains would be the most impressive real estate on which to erect an idol.[4] On a long journey, it wouldn't be unusual to see an idol or two casting a shadow over you as you trail through a valley. The Psalmist gazes upon an array of hilltop idols – all of which promise aid – and knows they won't deliver. He looks past these weathered and cracked false gods and sets his gaze upon the Lord.

There is something about looking up as we worship in a service. It's a natural inclination for our hearts to confess to God there is nothing around me that can do the job. Only the "Maker of heaven and earth" can carry us through this life. We can be confident in his ability to help because he made everything. He is the one who holds all things together (Col. 1:17) and promises he will never leave us (Heb 13:5). That is quite the combo. He makes some extraordinarily loving promises to us and has the muscle to back it up.

I wonder which part you struggle most to believe: that he is willing to help me or that he is able to. Both take a good amount of faith. You may be facing hard things you haven't brought to God because, truthfully, you can't imagine God doing anything about them. You may think you are unworthy because of your own failures, or you may weigh your problems against global catastrophes and assume God simply can't be bothered. On the flip side, maybe you have seen enough people die from cancer, marriages fail, or addictions take root that you start to believe God's help might be a nice spiritual sentiment rather than an actual intervention. Both kinds of doubt cause us to never reach out to the living God for help. Instead of burying these doubts, look to the Maker of heaven and earth and bring them to Him. Be honest with your hesitations, and ask him to help you see him as the ultimate source of help.

> Wounds from a friend can be trusted,
> but an enemy multiplies kisses.
>
> *PROVERBS 27:6*

LATELY, IT FEELS like ministry leaders are being disqualified on the regular. It's hard to say if this represents an actual increase in the failings of pastors, or if we're simply more aware of it. Regardless, as these troubling reports make their way into the mainstream and journalists sift through some of the ministerial debris, a common denominator emerges: a lack of accountability.

Part of being a disciple is being accountable. To be accountable is to continually preach to yourself of your need for other people; it's essential to meaningful progress in following Jesus. This runs counter to the cultural message that self-sufficiency and autonomy are signs of maturity. These markers move us closer to self-idolatry than Christian maturity. We need to examine our friendships and community. Do the closest people in your world have access to what churns under the surface of your life? Can anyone in your community group speak to your parenting? Can your spouse challenge your prayerlessness? Can your close friend push back on your gossip? Or have you fortified your ego from any loving confrontation? When guarding the ego, the stakes are high. Peter describes the devil as a prowling lion, waiting for someone to wander outside the camp (1 Peter 5:8). To receive "wounds from a friend" is to have him or her grab you by the collar and pull you back to the campfire. It might hurt, but being devoured by the lion hurts a lot more.

Many people these days want Jesus but not his church. Here's the thing: church is like a family dinner. No matter where the family is at, or what conflicts might be simmering, we come together to laugh, reminisce, tell stories, and feast. If you want christianity without the church, you are the teenager who takes dinner to their bedroom. You might be a part of the family, but all you catch are echoes of conversation down the hall. To open yourself – all of yourself – to close community is to make room for God to do a work in your life. It is worth asking, who are the people in your world that can encourage and challenge the most honest parts of you?

You prepare a table before me
in the presence of my enemies.
You anoint my head with oil;
my cup overflows.
Surely your goodness and love will follow me
all the days of my life,
and I will dwell in the house of the Lord forever.

PSALMS 23:5-6

THERE ISN'T MUCH about which we can proclaim "surely" these days. With a growing current of misinformation on our social media feeds, curated algorithms, a rise of conspiracy theories, and no shortage of YouTube voices to comment on the whole phenomena, we are left guessing about so much of what can actually be known in our world. Personally, my disoriented mind finds a place to hunker down in the words of King David, who was utterly convinced of one thing: that God's goodness and love will follow him everywhere. How is he so sure of this? David tells us in verse 5.

The Message translation says it this way: "You serve me a six-course dinner right in front of my enemies." God is so unbothered by the very real threat in David's life and that he feels it fitting to bring out the fine china and eat together. The imagery is amazing. God is always available for a quick bite, with eating together being a picture of meaningful and personal connection with his people. Regardless of whether you are in the throes of painful circumstances, high anxiety, or literal danger – the table is set.

And what happens around God's table?

God brings out the good stuff – the oil and the wine. The oil would be reserved for some of the most serious guests of honor. After traveling far, lounging back on the sofa and having fragrant oil poured over you would have been a fairly refreshing treatment. Then comes the wine, and it keeps coming. David says, "My cup overflows." To fill a guest's glass to the top is the host's subtle affirmation that the guest should make himself at home – that his presence is more than welcome. David is painting a picture of what intimacy with God looks like in his life: incredible, unrushed refreshment for his soul. David is convinced of God's goodness and love not because he read about it or heard about it, but because he made space to experience it. And what was available to David is available to you. In a world that has lost its sense of clarity and left you wanting, you can be sure there is a God who has already set the table for you.

The next day John was there again with two of his disciples. When he saw Jesus passing by, he said, "Look, the Lamb of God!" When the two disciples heard him say this, they followed Jesus. Turning around, Jesus saw them following and asked, "What do you want?" They said, "Rabbi" (which means "Teacher"), "where are you staying?" "Come," he replied, "and you will see." So they went and saw where he was staying, and they spent that day with him. It was about four in the afternoon.

JOHN 1:35-39

THE ONRAMPS INTO DISCIPLESHIP are usually pretty steep. It is not uncommon for Jesus to expect people to leave their families (Luke 14:26), abandon their businesses (Matt 4:22), or sell their possessions (Matt 19:21) to follow him. Yet, at this moment, he simply offers up a question: "What do you want?" It's interesting to see Jesus make space for those who are curious without requiring them to uproot their entire lives. Although it seems like a soft pitch, the question is really at the crux of all his encounters. He knows a complete reorientation must be made for us to detach from the world and follow him – not just a reorientation of thought and action, but also of desire. What we want drives the ship.

In the West, we see discipleship as primarily an intellectual endeavor. However, is knowledge really our biggest hang-up? When you sin, how often is it because you didn't know any better? Rarely. In reality, we are caught in our failures because we knew better, but wanted something different. If gaining more and more knowledge is our only strategy for spiritual formation, we will be left frustrated with our progress. James K Smith sums it up perfectly: "Jesus is a teacher who doesn't just inform our intellect but forms our very loves. He isn't content to simply deposit new ideas into your mind; he is after nothing less than your wants, your loves, your longings."[5] The work Jesus wants to do is deep and profound. He is not only convincing your mind, but wooing your heart to a life in the kingdom. That means you have to be willing to surrender your ideas of what St. Augustine calls "the good life."[6] To be intellectually convinced of something reasonable isn't that difficult. We exchange ideas, rethink viewpoints, and debate convictions all the time. However, to be wooed to a new vision for life and change your longings is like pulling out an old stump in the backyard – you just have to go deeper.

Have you ever stopped to question what your heart is chasing? Not what you think it should chase, but what is it actually chasing? It's not always easy to be honest with that question; however, to do so is to make an open space for the Spirit. Have you cognitively agreed with God's kingdom, but left your heart wandering the world? To forfeit our notions of the good life and yield to God's vibrant vision of the kingdom only happens in an honest and willing heart.

When Jesus saw his mother there, and the disciple whom he loved standing nearby, he said to her, "Woman, here is your son," and to the disciple, "Here is your mother." From that time on, this disciple took her into his home.

JOHN 19:26-27

JESUS MAKES SEVEN STATEMENTS while hanging from the cross. The ones that usually come to mind first are the powerful proclamations of "it is finished" and "forgive them for they do not know what they are doing." (Luke 23:34) Yet, with the little breath he has left, he also speaks words that are personal, intimate, and loaded with compassion. Jesus, knowing what it feels like to be cast aside by parts of his family (John 7:5), ensures this will not be the case for John and his mother. At the pinnacle of his suffering, as he struggles to hold his body up on the nails, Jesus' focus is on the needs of others. What a challenge for us today.

We are in a cultural moment where self-care and mental health are paramount concerns. In many ways, this is a healthy reaction to a workaholic culture driven by a compulsion for greater productivity. (It turns out that we have more complex needs than just food and sleep – who knew?!) However, with a surge of good intentions comes mixture. The drive to set rhythms and boundaries that sustain a balanced life has, however, become law for many. These systems can cause us to fixate on our own needs, protecting them at all costs. This, of course, becomes problematic when needs emerge around us. There is nothing wrong with prioritizing self-care, but we must discern when it becomes a masquerade for self-love.

In the book of Matthew, after learning about his cousin's death, Jesus retreats to grieve. Soon after, however, he is sought out by a crowd with great need. In this instance, Jesus is certainly entitled to some personal space and quiet time, but the text tells us "he had compassion on them" (Matt.14:13). He is willing to serve others when his emotional tank is empty. What is the challenge for us? To exhaust ourselves on the altar of ministry? No. It is to be mindful that mindfulness doesn't empower you to ministry, the Spirit does. God might want to use you when you are not at your best. You may not have a chance to retreat and recoup. You may even be in a place of great suffering. Yet, he reminds us, "My grace is sufficient for you, for my power is made perfect in weakness" (2 Cor. 12:9).

Where is he who set, his Holy Spirit among them,
who sent his glorious arm of power,
to be at Moses' right hand,
who divided the waters before them
like cattle that go down to the plain,
they were given rest by the Spirit of the Lord.
This is how you guided your people,
to make for yourself a glorious name.

ISAIAH 63:11-12, 14

WHAT COMES TO MIND when you think about the Holy Spirit? God sovereignly hovering over the creation of the world? A mighty wind invading the upper room? Or perhaps what hits home for you is William P. Young's image of an Asian female gardener tending to your soul, as described in *The Shack.*[7] Regardless of where your mind goes, there is an inescapable reality fundamental for the believer – the Holy Spirit resides in you (1 Cor. 3:16). The theological implications of that statement are vast and beautiful, but do you have an awareness of it in your day-to-day life? When is the last time you paused to consider who you are in business with?

In John 4:10, Jesus has one of his longest recorded conversations with a Samaritan woman who was pulling water from a well. Jesus uses the moment to offer her something much more profound than she expected – the Holy Spirit.[8] He observes, "If you knew the gift of God and who it is that asks you for a drink..." If she only knew.

But, if we are honest, do we know? In the back of our minds, the Holy Spirit sits in an abstract category. He occasionally offers up a sense of comfort and help when needed, but is that the full picture? Let's not move too fast past Isaiah's words.

It might not be obvious at first glance, but Isaiah is attributing the splitting of the Red Sea and the pillar of cloud and fire to the Holy Spirit. You remember, right? That chaotic pillar of wind and fire described as "billowing up like smoke from a furnace" and making Mount Sinai "tremble violently" (Exodus 19:18). Because of what Jesus accomplished, that unbridled force lives within you. That's a bit of a different perspective of who we are walking in step with. When we do an honest review of Jesus' call on our life, we often feel overwhelmed with the task. Certain sins are too ingrained in us to change. Certain expectations demand faith that just isn't there. We feel stuck in our walk with Jesus. Like the Samaritan woman, is it possible we don't quite realize what Jesus has on offer? As we strive to live out Jesus' plan for us, we need to trust that the Holy Spirit is capable of getting us there. Today, a first step might be to simply believe that the same Spirit who parted waters for a nation is able to make a way for what Jesus has for you this week.

"Is not my word like fire," declares the Lord, "and like a hammer that breaks a rock in pieces?

JEREMIAH 23:29

MANY CHRISTIANS TACKLE scripture devotionally; that is, they pick up a book similar to this one and carve out a couple minutes in the morning with an expectation to meet with God. That's good. We need to have consistent rhythms of uninterrupted time in God's word. But we also have to be careful regarding what we expect of that time. As Jen Wilkin notes, people often expect their time in scripture to "deliver a dose of emotional positivity before [they] head out into the world, all so that [the] day can be oriented properly."[9] What motivates us to pick up our Bibles?

Routine is a beautiful and a critical part of our spiritual formation, but it's not without its pitfalls. As a practice becomes second-nature to us, we can start to overlook what we have in our hands. Our devotional life can be reduced to capturing an inspirational passage and sharing it on social media. Without realizing it, that dose of positivity doesn't come from scripture, but from piety signaling on Instagram. Throughout history, the Bible has overturned governments, breathed life into cultures, dismantled unjust laws, burned down religious strongholds, and elevated the forgotten. This book is "like fire." That transformative power is available for our souls each morning. When we open God's word, we find it doesn't just inspire us, but purifies us by separating what is valuable from what is worthless (Isa. 1:25). Its agenda is to cut right through to the intentions of our heart (Heb. 4:12-14). That's a bit different from getting a boost of self-worth before starting the day.

Do the scriptures set out to encourage and uplift you? Absolutely. But let's not miss the power behind these words – words exclusively able to transform you into the image of Jesus. They are not only a comfort to your soul, but also a weapon against your flesh. When we consider what motivates us to pick up our Bibles, remember that this book isn't only about changing your outlook on the day, but changing the very person you are.

Hear this word, people of Israel, the word the Lord has spoken against you—against the whole family I brought up out of Egypt:

"You only have I chosen
of all the families of the earth;
therefore I will punish you
for all your sins."
Do two walk together
unless they have agreed to do so?

AMOS 3:1-3

IF MY SON LEARNS BAD BEHAVIORS on the playground and brings them home, it's my responsibility to take a knee, correct the behavior, remind him how our family operates, and affirm who he is. In this passage, God is taking a knee and talking to his children. He reminds Israel where they came from. As they sit pompously in their extravagant homes, God brings them back to the moment they were in Egypt sitting helplessly in chains. It didn't take long for them to lose their way, but God is gracious.

The verses that follow are peppered with questions, but the first one sets the tone. Most scholars think the question is a nod to Exodus 24, when God calls Moses to walk with him in covenant. To walk with God. Everyone has ideas of what this means. Some believe it's frantically trying to keep up as God sets an exhausting pace, continually looking back in disappointment. For others, they question the relevance of having the divine companion, an archaic guide who seems to slow down the pace. Still others are left wondering if God has become indifferent and abandoned the expedition completely. How we see God determines the pace we expect of ourselves. Perhaps what God offers us isn't a military march or an aimless saunter, but a dance.

We often see a father-daughter dance at a wedding. It is a vivid picture of parental love – decades of fatherly investment made clear on the dance floor. We feel the love, joy, laughter, and care, and hundreds of guests surrounding the dance floor get sucked into that love. (Strangers who came for the open bar are watching in tears, as the experience is for them, too). This was the call for God's people. Israel was invited to the dance floor to experience abundant fatherly love, learn the moves, and follow God's lead. The hope was subsequently for other nations to make their way around the dance floor and witness everlasting love between God and His people. All the people would be called to the dance floor.

We aren't Israelites, but we are God's people, and the invitation is the same. To walk with God is to allow him to take the lead on the floor. As we do, we discover radical love at the center of it – a love that doesn't stay contained between the two dancers, but overflows to those nearby. You can't give away what you have yet not experienced. Today, open yourself up to the abundant love of the Father for you.

> If any of you lacks wisdom, you should ask God,
> who gives generously to all without finding fault,
> and it will be given to you.
>
> *JAMES 1:5*

GOD HANDS OUT GENEROUSLY something of which we are always in short supply: wisdom. Here, James brings us back to an old Proverb: "The Lord gives wisdom" (Prov. 2:6). Seems like great news, but what exactly is it and how does God give it? JI Packer brings some clarity to the word: "Wisdom is the power to see and the inclination to choose the best and highest goal, together with the surest means of attaining it."[10] In short, wisdom directs the intention, means, and goal of every choice in your life. When it comes to God, Packer adds, "He alone is naturally and entirely and invariably wise."[11] God has never – and will never – make a decision that is inferior to the infinite possible alternatives. He is perfectly wise. And that same God makes it clear in James 1 that he is more than willing to lean in and give you some pointers.

Okay, so how do we access it? Well, in Luke 11, Jesus promises another gift to us: the Holy Spirit. One of the Spirit's primary jobs is to keep Jesus' teachings at the center of our lives (John 14:26). To make room for the Spirit or be led by the Spirit isn't simply to chase a spiritual experience, but to draw deeply from the well of God's wisdom. In a very real sense, the Spirit is our bucket. He is the one who guides us to Jesus – our teacher – and illuminates his perfect wisdom for our lives. If you ever doubt whether God cares enough to guide you to wisdom, just look to his Son. God generously gives wisdom because he generously gave Jesus. There is no one wiser who has set foot on this earth.

As you navigate a world of complex and morally-opaque choices, remember your teacher is at hand. Jesus delights in making you wise – not simply because it can prevent heartache in relationships, financial setbacks, or time spent in vain, but because it shapes you more into his image. We don't seek wisdom to get ahead, we seek it to look like Jesus. So ask for it, knowing the Holy Spirit leads you not to a solution, but a person.

Now when Jesus returned, a crowd welcomed him, for they were all expecting him. Then a man named Jairus, a synagogue leader, came and fell at Jesus' feet, pleading with him to come to his house because his only daughter, a girl of about twelve, was dying. As Jesus was on his way, the crowds almost crushed him... Hearing this, Jesus said to Jairus, "Don't be afraid; just believe, and she will be healed."

LUKE 8:40-42, 50

EACH OF JESUS' MIRACLES says something profound about the nature of God. Every miracle is a sermon that reverberates through the community revealing Jesus' mercy, power, compassion, authority, and, ultimately, his Godship. What I find fascinating is the type of miracles Jesus chooses to perform. There are infinite ways Jesus could demonstrate he is the Son of God, yet he chooses to spit in mud, curse a fig tree, walk on water, and cater a meal for five thousand. Although seemingly reactive and random, they are, in fact, sovereignly placed and timed interventions that speak about his kingdom. And it makes quite a statement that, of the twenty-three miracles documented in the Gospel of Luke, a handful of them involve kids.

Jesus hammers this home when his disciples try to dismiss a group of bothersome children and he rebukes them for doing so (Luke 18:16). Jesus welcomes the intrusion. For him, children are not a distraction, annoyance, or unwelcome presence, but a key demographic in his kingdom. It's not like he had extra time on his hands – remember, the "crowds almost crushed him." In this passage, we see many people with real needs who want his time and don't get it. Nevertheless, in the busyness of ministry, Jesus carves out space for the little ones.

As a parent, it's common to be concerned about the wellbeing of your kids. Are they safe? Who are they hanging out with? What are they watching? Why hasn't that cough gone away? If not in check, these worries can take up a lot of real-estate in our heads. Jairus comes to Jesus with no access to modern medicine. Even as an esteemed leader in the community, he isn't able to pull strings to help his dying daughter. Every parent can feel that moment where Jarius falls at the feet of Jesus as a last-ditch effort. And Jesus' words to Jarius resound for every parent in need: "Do not be afraid." The God who engineered the starry constellations and broke ground on the Himalayas cares about your daughter's rising fever. He is invested.

This doesn't negate the real suffering all around us. Yet, Jesus' words challenge us to not create a futile framework of parenting. We can't control what our children will face; but as parents, we can control whether we fall at the feet of Jesus. We can choose to entrust them to the one who delights in their presence.

On the third day a wedding took place at Cana in Galilee. Jesus' mother was there, and Jesus and his disciples had also been invited to the wedding. When the wine was gone, Jesus' mother said to him, "They have no more wine." "Woman, why do you involve me?" Jesus replied. "My hour has not yet come." His mother said to the servants, "Do whatever he tells you." Nearby stood six stone water jars, the kind used by the Jews for ceremonial washing, each holding from twenty to thirty gallons. Jesus said to the servants, "Fill the jars with water"; so they filled them to the brim. Then he told them, "Now draw some out and take it to the master of the banquet." They did so, and the master of the banquet tasted the water that had been turned into wine.

JOHN 2:1-9

MAYBE I'M GETTING OLD, but it takes a lot to get me on the dance floor these days. However, if there is a perfect storm of friends, music, and a prodding wife, that floor can draw me in. Weddings have a unique ability to do that. There is something about young love that is so easy to celebrate. In this text, Jesus and his disciples make their way to a wedding feast in the community. Yet, while the disciples are clinking glasses, eating good food, and breaking it down on the dance floor, Jesus is having a different moment. The celebration becomes a bit muted when the wine runs dry, and Mary expects Jesus to get involved. Jesus' response is a bit of a downer: "Woman, why do you involve me? My hour has not yet come." While everyone is living in the moment, Jesus has his mind on what is to come. Many believe being surrounded by the ecstatic joy of the wedding feast has Jesus thinking ahead to his own wedding. Relax, I'm not talking about the Da Vinci Code.[12] Scripture speaks of the future hope for God and his people to come together as the pinnacle of his redemptive story in the wedding feast (Rev. 19:7). The wedding preparations, however, are paved with Jesus' suffering on the cross. Edmund Clowney observes, "Jesus sat amidst all the joy sipping the coming sorrow, so that you and I today can sit amidst all this world's sorrow, sipping the coming joy." Joy is important to Jesus, and he is willing to pay a lot for us to have it.

You could argue joy is what propels Jesus towards his execution. Hebrews 12:2 makes a striking claim: "Looking to Jesus, the founder and perfecter of our faith, who for the joy that was set before him endured the cross." The Gospel of John shows Jesus' suffering intensifying as he draws near to the cross. However, his joy intensifies as well. The word "joy" is used twice in the first three quarters of the book; in the week leading up to his execution, it is used seven times. Jesus looks through the veil of death and sees God-glorifying joy on the other side. The call is for us to do the same. With estranged children, tragic medical reports, or unrelenting depression, we "can sit amidst all this world's sorrow, sipping the coming joy."

For Christ also suffered once for sins,
the righteous for the unrighteous,
that he might bring us to God, being
put to death in the flesh but made alive in the spirit.

1 PETER 3:18

I GET ROPED INTO A HUNTING TRIP with my family every few years. Five days in the middle of nowhere. It is always nice to see a bit of action in the bush, but the biggest appeal is being out in the stillness of nature – to detox from the frantic demands of life and recalibrate my priorities as a Jesus follower. As you walk through the dry, cold woods, it is not uncommon to come across a pile of bones or a half-eaten carcass. Even though you expect to encounter a dead animal as a hunter, it's a haunting experience, almost like evidence of an intruder on home soil.

As a pastor, I have walked alongside and through enough suffering to know death is no gentleman. It doesn't care if you loved or were loved, who you are leaving behind, or the untapped potential you might have. It doesn't honor your timing. It just takes. It does something within the individual that was never intended: disintegration. The body and soul, designed to make up the wholeness of a person, are ripped apart in the moment of death. The tragedy of death is something from which we run.

Jesus walks towards it.

No one coerced him. Jesus makes it clear: "No one takes it from me, but I lay it down of my own accord" (John 10:18). Death itself had no claim on him, since he was the only one in history who had never sinned. Death could not come to Jesus, so Jesus had to come to death. Why? "That he might bring us to God." Jesus steps into the execution room assigned for us. In the words of John Murray, "And as it were, Jesus Christ put one hand on his soul and one hand on his body and ripped himself apart."[13] Crass language, but no less true. God knows death.

By surrendering to death, Jesus, in turn, defangs his great enemy. This gives Paul the boldness to question what sting death has left (1 Cor. 15:55). We can walk in that same confidence. We follow the one who has conquered death on our behalf and invites us into a kingdom where it will one day be a faint memory. Knowing we are secure in Jesus and the life he has for us frees us from clinging to the offerings of this world. We don't have to squeeze out every moment for self-gratification, as if death lingers next door. We are preoccupied with pouring ourselves out for others, as Jesus has already claimed us for eternity.

Then he said to them, "The Sabbath was made for man, not man for the Sabbath. So the Son of Man is Lord even of the Sabbath."

MARK 2:27-28

MUCH WORK HAS GONE INTO understanding the differences between soldiers returning home from World War II and the Vietnam War. It was a polarizing outcome. The end of World War II ushered in a new era of national pride (and a lot of babies), while the Vietnam War brought about a catastrophic heroin epidemic. While there are plenty of factors that contributed to this, Dr. A.J. Swoboda identifies one that speaks right to our own spiritual formation. After the horrific events of the Vietnam War, soldiers were on a plane and back in their living rooms in two days flat. In contrast, it took months for soldiers of World War II to travel home by sea. Swoboda argues that what set those men up for success was having the time in their boats to grieve, heal, relate, and bond before re-entering society.[14] They had no option but to rest.

When we think about the Sabbath, we think about rest. The topic of the Sabbath is especially peppered throughout the Old Testament and is the only thing God claims as "holy" in the creation story, so it probably deserves some thought. Since we aren't bound to Israel's law, it would be tough to argue this is something legislated for Jesus' followers, but that doesn't mean we should ignore the concept entirely.

Why? Because Jesus says, “Sabbath was made for the man.”

Let’s be honest, we are unhinged. We have no framework for boundaries, limits, or rest. Our calendars are packed, our phone provides endless prompts, and the expectation for productivity has never been higher. But we kind of love it. There is a sense of purpose in being exhausted and strung out on work. However, what Jesus teaches and what World War II veterans reveal is that we are creatures of limitations.. We need space to step back, breathe, and enjoy some unhurried moments with God. For some, this is a moment to process and heal; for others, it is a time to worship and adore. Either way, these critical moments can only be completed in first gear. Think about it: when is the last time you were aware of God while rushed? Do you even have any margin to operate in a lower gear? Sabbath isn’t a duty. It is an invitation to slow down and rest in God’s presence – something for which we were all made.

The evening meal was in progress, and the devil had already prompted Judas, the son of Simon Iscariot, to betray Jesus. Jesus knew that the Father had put all things under his power, and that he had come from God and was returning to God; so he got up from the meal, took off his outer clothing, and wrapped a towel around his waist. After that, he poured water into a basin and began to wash his disciples' feet, drying them with the towel that was wrapped around him. He came to Simon Peter, who said to him, "Lord, are you going to wash my feet?" Jesus replied, "You do not realize now what I am doing, but later you will understand." "No," said Peter, "you shall never wash my feet."Jesus answered, "Unless I wash you, you have no part with me." "Then, Lord," Simon Peter replied, "not just my feet but my hands and my head as well!"

JOHN 13:2-9

WE CAN GLEAN A LOT FROM JUDAS' trajectory of betrayal and rejection. His life should flash as a warning sign for Christians because, at face value, he lives a better Christian life than most pastors we know. Tim Keller surveys the life of Judas and draws two conclusions. First, Judas had better input than any of us. He participated in the best small group experience, had a front-row seat to the best sermons in history, got to rub shoulders with the greatest moral example, and his ministry training would put any seminary to shame. Second, Judas had incredible output. Throughout the gospels, we are told all 12 disciples were sent out for impactful ministry. They all taught about the way of Jesus, evangelized to crowds, counseled the downcast, and miraculously healed the sick and cast out demons.[15] Judas didn't play hooky on these days; he was in the thick of some of the most vibrant ministry to date. With a resume like that, most churches would headhunt him in a heartbeat. Yet, an inspiring resume built over three years ended in betraying his Savior and hanging himself on a tree.

The life of Judas perfectly illustrates Jesus' warning in Matthew 7:22-23: "Many will say to me on that day, 'Lord, Lord, did we not prophesy in your name and in your name drive out demons and in your name perform many miracles?' 23 Then I will tell them plainly, 'I never knew you. Away from me, you evildoers!'" The word "many" should make all of us a little on edge. It is a reminder to carefully consider what exactly Jesus wants from us. Luckily, we find some strong indicators in Peter. The passage bounces back and forth between Peter and Judas, almost as a contrast between true and false discipleship. Judas makes it clear he wants no part of what Jesus offers. Peter is confronted with the same decision as Jesus kneels to wash his feet. Jesus states, "Unless I wash you, you have no part with me." Peter opts for a full scrub down – full surrender to Jesus. Surrender is rooted in the heart. Over the course of a meal, Judas completely closes his heart to Jesus, giving the devil a prime candidate with whom to work. Peter opens his heart as wide as possible.

Take a moment today to simply be still with your heart, and allow the Spirit to kindly redirect you to the one worthy of full surrender.

Just before dawn Paul urged them all to eat. "For the last fourteen days," he said, "you have been in constant suspense and have gone without food—you haven't eaten anything. Now I urge you to take some food. You need it to survive. Not one of you will lose a single hair from his head." After he said this, he took some bread and gave thanks to God in front of them all. Then he broke it and began to eat.

ACTS 27:33-35

THE MOST SIGNIFICANT ACTIONS can be overlooked if we don't catch what led up to them. In a vacuum, this passage looks like a quick dinner prayer. Paul, however, spends the previous few chapters in hell. The Jews see Paul as such a betrayal to Israel that many make an oath to not eat or drink until Paul was dead. He has to be one step ahead of each assassination attempt to simply share the good news. Eventually, the Sanhedrin are able to lawyer up (Acts 24:1) and drag Paul into the Roman legal machine. Completely innocent, he is now a prisoner of the Roman Empire. His ministry was now wrapped up in politics and courtrooms. Governor Felix deflects the case to Festus, who quickly throws it to King Agrippa, who, like the rest, can't find fault in Paul, so he places him in jail for two years to buy time. Being the PR nightmare he is, Paul is thrown around like a ragdoll defending himself in front of judge after judge. Finally, they wash their hands of him and send him to the courts of Caesar in Rome. With over 250 other prisoners, the ship pushes past the advised sailing season and tackles the winter seas. Paul and the men endure a nightmare of a voyage. Continually on the verge of a shipwreck, a prisoner uprising, and starvation, Paul helps the ship finally make it to Malta. And the night before they crash their ship onto the shores – in the thick of the chaos – Paul pulls the men together, picks up a loaf of bread, and gives thanks to God.

It's one thing to say thank you when you are sitting comfortably on the couch; but when you are soaking wet, starving, and not sure if you are going to survive the night, it leaves a different impression of heaven. In the violent storm, Paul is grateful. You can't fake that. Pain, suffering, betrayal, isolation, and loss hook into Paul and peel him back layer after layer; what is left was a man utterly fixed on Jesus. When life squeezes us, what comes out? Some would argue it's our truest self. That's the thing about suffering: it's revealing. On our own, this would be very humbling. But remember, we hide ourselves within the one who endured the full measure of pain and suffering. When the whole world pressed down on him, the sweetest words poured out of him: "Father, forgive them, for they do not know what they are doing" (Luke 23:34). When our wicked hearts are revealed, they are met with Christ's forgiving heart.

Someone in the crowd said to him, "Teacher, tell my brother to divide the inheritance with me." Jesus replied, "Man, who appointed me a judge or an arbiter between you?" Then he said to them, "Watch out! Be on your guard against all kinds of greed; life does not consist in an abundance of possessions."

LUKE 12:13-15

WE ARE A CULTURE THAT LOVES STUFF. Everyone knows what materialism is. Everyone knows what greed is. However, the real question that plagues every Christian is knowing where the line is. At what point do you have too much stuff or too much in savings? And how do you know if you have crossed that line? In her research, Jan Johnson states: "Only one-third of American households that make more than $100,000 a year agree with the statement, 'I can afford to buy everything I really need.'"[16] The wealthiest people in the wealthiest country in the history of the world believe they can't afford everything they really need. Wherever the line is, most of us have no idea how to find it.

In this passage, the man in the crowd gets tripped up by the same lure that is common to all of us: he wants to use Jesus to acquire more wealth for himself. As he is trying to leverage the Rabbi's position to squeeze more money out of his family, he doesn't see the glaring blind spot in his own soul. He is looking in the eyes of truth and feels righteous indignation in wanting more. Like this man, we all tend to draw the line for greed just beyond where we currently see ourselves. We look at our neighbor's new pool and our coworker's new car and are convinced it is not our issue. Yet, any unattended heart will gravitate towards covetousness. AW Tozer explains:

> There is within the human heart a tough fibrous root of fallen life whose nature is to possess, always to possess. It covets things with a deep and fierce passion... and we dare not pull up one rootlet lest we die. Things have become necessary to us, a development never originally intended. God's gifts now take the place of God, and the whole course of nature is upset with the monstrous substitution.[17]

The issue comes down to idolatry. The heart is moved by the hollow promises wealth offers us, and the only real shot we have of resisting their pull is to submit our hearts to the care of the Great Physician. It is only by his surgical hands the "tough, fibrous roots" are removed. In reality, greed isn't an amount: it's a condition. A condition only Jesus can remedy. Tozer calls out our fear of pulling up rootlets, but that may be the very thing the Great Physician calls all of us to do: to go under the knife and emerge as a new person with a new heart.

As Peter entered the house, Cornelius met him and fell at his feet in reverence. But Peter made him get up. "Stand up," he said, "I am only a man myself."... On the appointed day Herod, wearing his royal robes, sat on his throne and delivered a public address to the people. They shouted, "This is the voice of a god, not of a man." Immediately, because Herod did not give praise to God, an angel of the Lord struck him down, and he was eaten by worms and died.

ACTS 10:25-26, 12:21-23

WE ALL ENJOY PRAISE. Affirmation, honor, and encouragement should abound in the church body. However, they make a terrible mortar for the foundation of your identity. Wrapping your personhood around the words of others can become an insatiable need. Take Herod, for example. Despite his power and recognition, he still craves more. Here he stands before the people and receives a full dose of adulation. Celebrated as a God, the alluring praise is too sweet to resist, and the fear of utter blasphemy is drowned out by the roaring crowd. But, God will not be mocked, and he strikes down this false deity. It's a harsh reminder that a life revolving around self-glorification inevitably pushes God out of orbit – and, at some point, that void is filled with death.

It is no coincidence this passage sits on the backdrop of Peter's encounter. Where Herod allows the worship to ring on and on, Peter immediately gets down to Cornelius' level and calls him to stand as his equal. Through the Spirit, Peter conquers his appetite for self-glorification. His identity isn't built on ego, reputation or a need for praise, it's anchored in Christ. In other words, he's not really into himself.

Consider another ego-slayer: John the Baptist. He was emptied of his popularity and influence as soon as Jesus came on the scene. The same crowds who wondered if John himself was the Messiah jumped ship and joined Jesus' entourage within a few days (John 3:25). Where most would scramble to hold onto any sense of influence or reputation, John is so stable in his God-given identity that he sees the whole ordeal as joyous.

We like to aspire to John's words: "He must become greater, I must become less." But so often, our mantra devolves to I must become greater so I can make him greater. The desire to be liked, influential, and popular is easily masked under the umbrella of having a greater impact for Jesus. To become less seems counterintuitive to the mission. But John and Peter don't see it that way. They are reluctant to leverage opportunities to become something more, even as the crowds lay opportunities ahead of them. They make little of themselves and much of Jesus. Perhaps the call for us is to become less. Not to fill our lives laboring toward a personal empire, but being assured participants in a kingdom Christ has already built.

Should nothing of our efforts stand, No legacy survive,
Unless the Lord does raise the house, In vain its builders strive.
To you who boast tomorrow's gain, Tell me, what is your life?

A mist, it vanishes at dawn, All glory be to Christ.[18]

I have perfumed my bed
with myrrh, aloes and cinnamon.
Come, let's drink deeply of love till morning;
let's enjoy ourselves with love!
My husband is not at home;
he has gone on a long journey.
He took his purse filled with money
and will not be home till full moon."
With persuasive words she led him astray;
she seduced him with her smooth talk.
All at once he followed her
like an ox going to the slaughter,
like a deer stepping into a noose
till an arrow pierces his liver,
like a bird darting into a snare,
little knowing it will cost him his life.

PROVERBS 7:17-23

THIS GAL IS OFFERING ALL the trimmings: perfumes, oils, and secrecy. That little piece of propaganda hasn't changed over the course of human history; lust promises ecstatic pleasure with no consequences. Our current hypersexualized culture takes it a step further. The messaging today is Why hide what's not wrong? Open relationships, pornography in the marriage bed, or sexting pictures to strangers are all an affront on what culture sees as outdated and oppressive boundaries; carnal appetites are not meant to be overcome, but normalized and experienced. In this passage, the woman[19] at the door champions the destruction of any healthy constraints on human sexuality. She is the preacher in the town square who proclaims self-indulgence.

What is left in the wake of this destruction? As a pastor, I can confidently tell you the remaining verses aren't an overstatement. Not only are families, marriages, and friendships caught in the blast radius, but also your soul (1 Cor 6:18), and, most importantly your walk with Jesus (1 Cor 6:9). What starts with the mind enjoying the scents of "myrrh, aloes and cinnamon" ends with a life in ruins.

What is the way forward for us? Well, it's worth mentioning that temptation is a lot easier to overcome when you aren't sitting on the edge of the bed. Proverbs 5 hits it straight on: don't even go near her house. Don't entertain, manage, or excuse sexual sin. Stay out of earshot of the "smooth talk" and don't let the perfumes make their way over. At risk of sounding religious or legalistic, we should unapologetically have some clear boundaries for ourselves. Each person is different, but we can't aimlessly wander the streets hoping we don't catch wind of the scents.

For those who have their scars from the "snare" and "noose," there may be deeper layers of healing, confession, and even counseling needed, but there is hope. In the gospels, we read of another woman who probably would have been pegged as a Proverbs 7 kind of gal in her community. She knows the cheap promises of "drinking deeply of love till morning." With a terrible reputation, she encounters Jesus at a well. Regardless of her moral standing, he offers her a different drink that "will become in [her] a spring of water welling up to eternal life" (John 4:14).

Then James and John, the sons of Zebedee, came to him. "Teacher," they said, "we want you to do for us whatever we ask." "What do you want me to do for you?" he asked. They replied, "Let one of us sit at your right and the other at your left in your glory." "You don't know what you are asking," Jesus said... When the ten heard about this, they became indignant with James and John. Jesus called them together and said, "You know that those who are regarded as rulers of the Gentiles lord it over them, and their high officials exercise authority over them. Not so with you.

MARK 10:35-38, 41-43

HAVE YOU EVER HAD THAT MOMENT of anticipation around your boss? When an opportunity has arisen in the office and a handful of people can smell it in the air? Perhaps there is a chance to take the lead on an ambitious project, offer fresh new management to a key department, or a corner office has just become available. These tokens of power can steer our priorities easily.

Now, there is nothing wrong with power itself – it is the source and use of that power that matters. Jamin Goggin and Kyle Strobel are convinced the letter of James[20] only sees power from two places: the way below or the way above.[21] The way below uses power to make oneself great. It's guided by the flesh and resonates with the world. In contrast, the way above allows God to powerfully work through our weakness for the sake of others. The reason the way below is so enticing for us is because it works. Money seems to get better results than prayer, charisma wins people over quicker than sacrificial love, and career accolades are more impressive than being the least of these. It is why in Matthew 16:22, Peter has a problem with Jesus' strategy for building his kingdom. Dying is not powerful, especially when Jesus is riding the pinnacle of his influence. This bothers Peter so much that he confronts Jesus. After calling Peter "Satan," Jesus declares: "You are not setting your mind on the things of God, but on the things of man." Peter wants to get things done with the power below. He is not alone in this. James and John want top tier authority in eternity. They make their pitch for exclusive seats of power, and subsequently the other eavesdropping disciples become hungry for the same. Just like the colleague who wines and dines the boss to make his pitch for the corner office before you do, the remaining disciples are indignant that James and John make the bold ask first. Yet, Jesus sits all of them down and paints a different vision of power: one that is not self-serving and domineering like that of the Gentile lords and high officials.

The way above follows the 2 Corinthians 13:4 flow of power: "He was crucified in weakness, yet he lives by God's power. Likewise, we are weak in him, yet by God's power we will live with him." It is by embracing the cross that God's power moves through us. Just look at the kinds of people who get power in God's kingdom: the meek (Matt 5:5), the humble (Matt 23:12), the last (Matt 20:16), and those who lose their lives (Matt 10:39). Jesus makes it clear to his disciples that there is no room for ego or selfish ambition in this vision of power.

Think about your life and your circles of influence. How are you using your power? Are you driven by posturing yourself as impressive, using people to get what you want and subtly lording it over friends and family? Or are you following in the steps of Jesus, embracing weakness, praying simply (Matt 6:8), giving secretly (Matt 6:4), and serving the least of these (Matt 25:40) all for the sake of love? That is true power.

Some men came carrying a paralyzed man on a mat and tried to take him into the house to lay him before Jesus. When they could not find a way to do this because of the crowd, they went up on the roof and lowered him on his mat through the tiles into the middle of the crowd, right in front of Jesus. When Jesus saw their faith, he said, "Friend, your sins are forgiven."

LUKE 5:18-20

THERE IS AN INTERESTING juxtaposition in this passage: we witness a proactive effort to participate in the solution mixed with utter dependence on God to do the impossible. The paralyzed man and his friends observe a packed room; and although Jesus has performed some long-distance miracles (Luke 7:1-10), these men do not sit back with a posture of if it's meant to happen, it'll happen. They persistently and creatively participate in the miracle. Sometimes we think action is at odds with faith. If we take matters into our own hands, we are not trusting God. On the contrary, inaction can be evidence of weak faith. These men are so convinced Jesus can help that they are willing to destroy their neighbor's roof, tarnish their reputation with the local religious leaders, and interrupt Jesus' teaching. These are actions not opposed to faith, but infused with it. As they lower their friend on a makeshift gurney, Jesus sees their faith and honors it. Weak faith, on the other hand, would have left them outside the house.

Dallas Willard provides a similar thought, "Grace is not opposed to effort, it is opposed to earning. Earning is an attitude. Effort is an action."[22] We don't put effort into the problem to twist God's arm to action, as if we are owed some supernatural response. That's transactional. We put effort in because God calls us to participate in what he is doing. That's relational. How do you primarily relate to the idea of faith? It's often seen as something to wield against our problems. Our faith marinates our situation in the hope God will bring about a positive outcome. This approach centers our faith around the problem, fixated on it changing. Perhaps it's more helpful to see faith as a gravitational pull that draws you to the center of all things: God. The faith of these men pulls them into God's orbit.

Don't get me wrong – there are plenty of challenges in this life so beyond our control that the only possible action is prayer. However, it's worth asking: are you looking at your situation and leaning back – expecting God to move all the pieces – or do you see an invitation to participate in what God is doing? Is faith mobilizing you? Is it pulling you into the center?

Yet this I call to mind and therefore I have hope: Because of the Lord's great love we are not consumed, for his compassions never fail. They are new every morning; great is your faithfulness. I say to myself, The Lord is my portion; therefore I will wait for him.

LAMENTATIONS 3:22-23

THIS PASSAGE SITS AGAINST the backdrop of Jerusalem's destruction. Jerusalem symbolized everything for the Jewish people. God's fulfilled promises and future hopes were represented in each street paved and building erected. But because of idolatrous decisions, they sit in the debris of their consequences. The book of Lamentations rings true for a people who lost everything. In great loss, they reach out for the only hope they have: God's great and compassionate love.

The expression "great love" (hesed) is also infused with kindness and loyalty. As one author expands, "Hesed is the kind of act that is not required by civil law but springs from the concerned character of the one who acts."[23] God binds us in his covenantal love not out of duty, but because it is his nature to do so. We can't do anything to better posture ourselves for receiving his compassion. That is difficult to accept when you are in the thick of it. When your prayer life is abysmal, you have made a mess of friendships or left people in the wake of your career success, you can't cover up your sin to better access his great love. You can only do what the Jews did: sitting in the ashes of their idolatry, they cling to the unchanging nature of God.

One of the most frequently preached passages in the Bible is the story of Jesus calming the storm in the boat. Pastors often allegorize the storm as modern-day circumstances or challenges that happen to us, but it's important to know our compassionate God also calms storms we have personally stirred up. When we obsess over fixing our own disasters before seeking God's great love, we miss the whole picture. You cannot earn that kind of love – you can only receive it. Desmond Tutu states, "Like when you sit in front of a fire in winter – you are just there in front of the fire. You don't have to be smart or anything. The fire warms you."[24] Regardless of whether life is happening to you or you are making a mess of it, come to Jesus. Know that His great love and compassion "are new every morning."

This is how we know what love is: Jesus Christ laid down his life for us. And we ought to lay down our lives for our brothers and sisters. If anyone has material possessions and sees a brother or sister in need but has no pity on them, how can the love of God be in that person? Dear children, let us not love with words or speech but with actions and in truth.

1 JOHN 3:16-18

WHEN YOU THINK ABOUT the Dead Sea, you probably think about a bunch of tourists floating around. As the final stop for the Jordan River, the sea contains an excessive amount of salt that makes everything buoyant. It is a place into which life flows, but nothing flows back out. It has become a salty graveyard for anything living.

In this passage, John tries to show us the natural flow of the gospel. Since Jesus has laid down his life for us, we ought to do the same for others. Have you seen that flow in your life? Often we frame the health of our soul based on our own needs. The primary strategy seems to be pouring life inward; honestly, most churches and events are marketed to that tune. Yet, as Paul reminds us, "Christ's love compels us" to look outward (2 Cor. 5:14). That word "compels" has some serious overlap with the word "controls." The potent seed of the gospel in our hearts has no choice but to produce bountiful fruit in our lives. The abounding love of God poured over us, and spilled into our friends, family, and community.

Unlike the Dead Sea, God's love doesn't flow into our lives and settle into salty waters, but rather breaks through dry barriers and carves out new streams for others to enjoy. It compels you to serve people you would typically overlook. Its aim is outward. So, examine your life. Be diligent in allowing God to continually pour into you – it's essential. After all, the Dead Sea would be a barren desert if it wasn't for the Jordan River's current. But the question remains: is your life producing new streams for others to experience the love of Jesus? Have you carved out avenues for your life to be poured out to others?

On the next Sabbath almost the whole city gathered to hear the word of the Lord. When the Jews saw the crowds, they were filled with jealousy. They began to contradict what Paul was saying and heaped abuse on him. Then Paul and Barnabas answered them boldly: "We had to speak the word of God to you first. Since you reject it and do not consider yourselves worthy of eternal life, we now turn to the Gentiles.

ACTS 13:44-46

IT NEVER FEELS GOOD when someone steps into your territory. The religious leaders and devout jews of Antioch want nothing more than to see a greater commitment to the synagogue and the law from the people. However, over the course of a few days, the winds have changed and the entire city turns their attention to two unassuming preachers: Paul and Barnabas. The passion and curiosity they were hoping to see in the people has found its place in something new. The way of Jesus is now a threat; and instead of keeping soft inquisitive hearts, the religious leaders harden them with jealousy.

Jealousy has a bigger explosive radius in our souls than we may think. For the Jews, jealousy was enough of a deterrent that they stared good news right in the face and turned it down. Scripture continually warns us about the impact of jealousy, especially in the book of James. James pulls no punches where jealousy is concerned, calling it "demonic, earthly and unspiritual." He then reiterates, "For where you have envy and selfish ambition, there you find disorder and every evil practice" (James 3:16). When have you ever made a wise decision while jealous? When have your relationships prospered? When have you felt close to God? We know jealousy has a viral effect, so why do we allow it free reign in our lives? Because jealousy is deceptive in appearance. Jaquelle Crowe reminds us, "Jealousy pretends to be a friend. It wants to sympathetically vindicate your sinful feelings by fostering discontentment and self-pity."[25] It's not always easy to catch its corrosive effects because when our hearts are drowning in envy, the twisted vindication can be satisfying.

So, how do we shake off this unwanted companion? The obvious solution is to look at what Jesus has placed in your hands. That is easier said than done. After the resurrection, Jesus has this beautiful and personal encounter with Peter, reinstating him and calling him to greater leadership (John 21). Yet, the first question out of Peter's mouth is about the fate of another disciple. Jesus corrects his immediate comparison by stating, "You must follow me." Jealousy dissolves when we focus on Jesus instead of looking around the room. Being earnestly faithful to the gift or task Jesus gives us provides clarity and keeps disorder at bay.

People will be lovers of themselves, lovers of money, boastful, proud, abusive, disobedient to their parents, ungrateful, unholy, without love, unforgiving, slanderous, without self-control, brutal, not lovers of the good, treacherous, rash, conceited, lovers of pleasure rather than lovers of God— having a form of godliness but denying its power. Have nothing to do with such people. They are the kind who worm their way into homes and gain control over gullible women, who are loaded down with sins and are swayed by all kinds of evil desires, always learning but never able to come to a knowledge of the truth. Just as Jannes and Jambres opposed Moses, so also these teachers oppose the truth. They are men of depraved minds, who, as far as the faith is concerned, are rejected. But they will not get very far because, as in the case of those men, their folly will be clear to everyone.

2 TIMOTHY 3:2-9

ODD PASSAGE. Here we have some heretical smooth talkers preying on a group of vulnerable women. It probably needs to be clarified that Paul isn't making a sweeping statement about women in general. This unique group is most likely new to the faith; being "loaded down with sins" may be a nod to a past of religious perversion or prostitution. Although the primary charge is against the men, there are warnings for us in how Paul describes these women.

If we aren't, we can find ourselves just as receptive to false, but compelling, ideas.

There are a few roadblocks in place that derail these women from truly being planted in the gospel. First is shame. These ladies are "loaded down with sins;" shame lodged in the body for years causes us to become receptive to ideas that diminish or excuse past sins. Ideas that sanctify us not by the way of the cross, but by denial of sin and its effects. It's the back alley approach to wholeness, and it doesn't work. Nevertheless, we are quick to entertain it because shame is a powerful feeling and many of us are willing to bend the truth to curb it. In order for truth to stay on the throne of our hearts, shame must be dealt with graciously and swiftly at the feet of Jesus.

Secondly, these women were "swayed by all kinds of evil desires" and "various passions."[26] Shame isn't the only threat to truth: our flesh is continually trying to chip away at it as well. The sweetest words our flesh can hear are the serpent's challenge in the garden: "Did God really say..." (Gen 3:1). Where shame works at the backend denying the corrosive effects of sin, our flesh works on the front end denying God's standards for holiness. We must be sober-minded about our unique proclivities and tighten up the reins where it matters.

Lastly, these women are arrogant. Paul distinctly points out that they are "always learning but never able to come to a knowledge of the truth." Their appetite for learning fools them into thinking they could never be deceived. The breadth of knowledge they carry has become their safeguard. It is a recipe for disaster.

For the last two millennia, Paul has called all of us to "work out [our] own salvation with fear and trembling" (Phil 2:12). There is a reason for that. Keeping truth permeating in our hearts isn't a natural inclination. It takes reverence and humility. Thankfully we are not alone in this endeavor. We are to "guard it with the help of the Holy Spirit who lives in us." (2 Tim. 1:14)

The heavens declare the glory of God;
the skies proclaim the work of his hands.
Day after day they pour forth speech;
night after night they reveal knowledge.
They have no speech, they use no words;
no sound is heard from them.
Yet their voice goes out into all the earth,
their words to the ends of the world.

PSALMS 19:1-4

FULL CONFESSION: I DONT always have my eyes on the road when driving through a nice neighborhood or the heart of downtown. Something in me loves the intentional design and form of architecture; it is a flex of humankind's technical and creative muscles for everyone to see. I marvel at those achievements alongside a voice in my head that asks, What can't we do? Recently, I saw a picture of Mount Everest's peak showing dozens of climbers waiting in line for their turn to have a moment at the top. Climbing Mount Everest was once seen as a life-defining achievement, but now many climbers set their sights on tackling the eleven highest mountains in one lifetime. For them, Mount Everest simply checks one of many boxes.

Our ambition seems to be progressing at a wild rate! However, we put ourselves in a dangerous spot when we conclude nothing is beyond our reach. I once heard a pastor say he intentionally spends time in nature away from his home in New York City as a sort of recalibration: a shift to being in awe of God's creation instead of man's. He recognizes that to have a life saturated by human achievement is to miss a component of what it means to be truly human. We don't need hiking boots and a Patagonia vest to find God, but something is at work when we surround ourselves with his raw materials. To become tunnel-visioned in your own achievement can only produce an inflated sense of self-importance; broadening our vision of the vast world God created situates us in a proper posture of dependency. After all, we are ourselves creatures in the grand scheme of things, something very much felt when lying in the dark gazing at the starry abyss above.

Tim Keller observes, "Without a powerful sense of God's reality, good circumstances can lead to overconfidence and spiritual indifference." As Christians, we strive to live in step with God's reality, and I think, in part, that involves getting out of our city. Are there small ways today you can be in awe of God's creation?

When Martha heard that Jesus was coming, she went out to meet him, but Mary stayed at home. "Lord," Martha said to Jesus, "if you had been here, my brother would not have died. But I know that even now God will give you whatever you ask." Jesus said to her, "Your brother will rise again." Martha answered, "I know he will rise again in the resurrection at the last day." Jesus said to her, "I am the resurrection and the life. The one who believes in me will live, even though they die; and whoever lives by believing in me will never die. Do you believe this?" "Yes, Lord," she replied, "I believe that you are the Messiah, the Son of God, who is to come into the world." After she had said this, she went back and called her sister Mary aside. "The Teacher is here," she said, "and is asking for you." When Mary heard this, she got up quickly and went to him. Now Jesus had not yet entered the village, but was still at the place where Martha had met him. When the Jews who had been with Mary in the house, comforting her, noticed how quickly she got up and went out, they followed her, supposing she was going to the tomb to mourn there. When Mary reached the place where Jesus was and saw him, she fell at his feet and said, "Lord, if you had been here, my brother would not have died."

JOHN 11:20-32

LAZARUS, A GOOD FRIEND OF JESUS, has just died. This reality is not sitting well with his two sisters, Mary and Martha. They realized Lazarus' health was deteriorating quickly, but had seen enough of Jesus' miracles and heard of how much he cared for the sick to be convinced he would intervene. Based on past experiences, they not only expected Jesus could save Lazarus, but would. After Jesus shows up too late, you can hear the frustration and confusion: "If you had been here, my brother would not have died." They were disappointed in God.

Have you been there? Challenging moments in which you believe God can easily intervene, but doesn't in the way you had hoped? A health issue in the family that doesn't move in the right direction. A foreclosure on the house. A marriage that slowly dissolves. In the thick of these moments, you have the same gut-wrenching disappointment as Mary and Martha. The struggle with this mystery is not one the Bible ignores. The Psalmist cries out, "Will you forget me forever? How long will you hide your face from me?" (Ps 13:1). Even the famous apologist C.S. Lewis laments after the death of his wife, "Go to Him when your need is desperate, when all other help is vain, and what do you find? A door slammed in your face, and a sound of bolting and double bolting on the inside. After that, silence."[28] The notion of being forsaken can be paralyzing.

In this dire moment, Jesus identifies the underlying doubts, fears, and frustrations raging in Mary and Martha. Jesus first converses back and forth with Martha, assuring her that she is looking in the eyes of resurrection life. He later moves to Mary and, knowing her needs in that moment are vastly different, simply sits down and weeps alongside her. Lazarus would be peeling off grave clothes in mere minutes, but the women had what they needed in that moment. They didn't get the explanations for which they longed; instead, they got Jesus, and it was personal. I think that is all we can hope for. Lewis reaches the same conclusion: questions will linger on this side of eternity, but that doesn't mean we have been forsaken. He closes his book, "When I lay these questions before God I get no answer. But a rather special sort of 'No answer.' It is not the locked door. It is more like a silent, certainly not uncompassionate, gaze. As though He shook His head not in refusal but waving the question. Like, 'Peace, child: you don't understand."

> You did not choose me, but I chose you and appointed you so that you might go and bear fruit—fruit that will last—and so that whatever you ask in my name the Father will give you.
>
> *JOHN 15:16*

LET'S NOT GIVE OURSELVES too much credit. Jesus came down the mountain to get us, not the other way around. But look at the text: God doesn't just choose us for salvation, with all its justifying and liberating benefits, but appoints us. That means there is a tailored and personal call to Jesus' mission. He hands us an assortment of spiritual gifts, instills in us unique kingdom passions, and sends us off. As Paul likens us to parts of the body, it's important to know we all bring something different and needed to the table (1 Cor 12:20). Taking time to discover your God-ordained sweet spot takes some effort. It usually involves prayer, the voice of mature believers, and a lot of trial and error. Yet, pinpointing the passions and gifts God is forming in you is only half the battle. Settling into it can be a whole new journey with Jesus.

John Ortberg identifies three categories of abilities in everyone's life. The first is our strengths.[29] Quite obviously, these are the skills and gifts that have become second nature to us. The second category is our weaknesses. We have come to a point in our lives where we don't feel a need to be excellent at everything. We have narrowed our skill set and are comfortable not being proficient at what others have mastered. Then there is the third category: the weaknesses we have an emotional need to be strengths.

We often hear of people who never saw leadership in themselves, but have this amazing raw potential in them pulled forth by the Spirit. Equally as beautiful are the untold stories of those who feel an unhealthy need to find their value in leadership but hear the Spirit gently say, This isn't what I have for you. He underburdens us from these self-induced pressures that simmer under the surface. When you shed unhelpful expectations and focus on settling into God-appointed ones, your attention goes to what matters: bearing fruit. No matter what shape and form that fruit takes, if God is the one who has appointed you to bear it, what else matters?

"Go down, sit in the dust,
Virgin Daughter Babylon;
sit on the ground without a throne,
queen city of the Babylonians.
No more will you be called tender or delicate.
Take millstones and grind flour; take off your veil.
Lift up your skirts, bare your legs, and wade through
the streams. Your nakedness will be exposed and your
shame uncovered. I will take vengeance;
I will spare no one." Our Redeemer—
the LORD Almighty is his name—
is the Holy One of Israel.
"Sit in silence, go into darkness,
queen city of the Babylonians;
no more will you be called queen of kingdoms.

ISAIAH 47:1-5

WHEN I WAS 16, I had the opportunity to go to Venice on a school band trip. (I have no idea what it had to do with learning saxophone, but I wasn't going to miss that opportunity). Venice is beautiful, and it was easy to get caught up in the architecture and ambiance of the place. But as we walked across metal-grated sidewalks, I was reminded the city is sinking. With rising tides and sinking foundations, experts forecast much of the city will be underwater in a century. It's what one journalist calls the "Damnation of

Venice."[30] Even though the city presents itself as vibrant and lively, it can't escape its inevitable watery grave.

Isaiah makes the same claim about Babylon.

While the nation plays a key role at one point in Israel's history, it represents a broader influence on humankind. Babylon's origins lay in the hearts of men who had the vision to build a tower for their namesake (Gen. 11:4). Although God puts a supernatural stop work order on Babel, the vision for self-exalting kingdoms has been pervasive across history. The Babylonian vision has influenced art, politics, education, business, family, and even religion. Yet, Isaiah makes it clear God's vision for humanity is counter to that of Babylon, and he will one day bring down the city's power.

Although the city is sinking, its vision is all around us. There is no real escaping its influence on our daily life. In reality, everyone has succumbed to Babylon, except one. At the beginning of Jesus' ministry, he is led into the wilderness. At Jesus' weakest point, the Devil offers all the Babylon-infused kingdoms of the world to Jesus and he doesn't bite. He rebukes the Devil and leaves the wilderness, inviting people into a different kingdom (Mark 1:14).

Here is our hope. Because of Jesus' victory in the desert, he has carved a path for us to resist Babylon. As we walk in step behind Jesus, the Spirit transforms us by the renewing of our minds (Rom. 12:2). We detox from the Babylonian vision as we begin to be compelled by Jesus'. This doesn't happen overnight; yet, through a daily rhythm of connecting with our Savior, we begin to see the world as it ought to be. This vision begins to move our hearts to seek the well-being of others rather than building kingdoms for ourselves. It is worth taking a moment to discern where you feel your heart is being pulled – towards the City of God or the City of Babylon.

The LORD is my light and my salvation - whom shall I fear? The LORD is the stronghold of my life - of whom shall I be afraid? When evil men advance against me to devour my flesh, when my enemies and my foes attack me, they will stumble and fall.

PSALMS 27:1-2

THE LIFE OF A CHRISTIAN is one driven by love. This sounds like it should be easy, but it's not. We live in a world marked by division, hatred, and violence. The global wars, genocide, and racial riots we see on the news grow from the same roots as the cynicism, gossip, jealousy, and bitterness we find in our churches and families. Undergirding the pain we see in so many forms is one common denominator: fear. For Christians desiring to expand their love for others, fear is the current that smashes against our best intentions. It's not surprising that "do not be afraid" is the most repeated commandment in the Bible.

Henri Nouwen states, "As we keep our eyes directed at the One who says, ''Do not be afraid,' we may slowly let go of our fear. We will learn to live in a world without zealously defended borders. We will be free to see the suffering of other people, free to respond not with defensiveness, but with compassion, with peace, with ourselves".[31] This is, according to Nouwen, one of our primary spiritual tasks: moving from the House of Fear to the House of Love. We can't live in both. This task becomes increasingly challenging as we grow old. In our youth, we are much more open-handed with trust, have less to lose, remain hopeful of what can be, and don't yet carry scars of failure. As life moves along, it becomes easier to remain in the House of Fear. So, how do we tackle this great spiritual task and become a resident of the House of Love?

This passage reminds us that the Lord is our fear detox. There is nothing in ourselves that can resist the current of fear that washes over us. It is only by abiding in the one who is love that fear falls to the wayside. It is only by being in communion with the Lord of light that cynicism, bitterness, and jealousy dissipate into darkness. All of this happens in prayer. Every time we open ourselves up to prayer, God re-invites us back into the House of Love. It is his home. Today, pray you would enter his home, experience his love, and hold fast to this question: "whom shall I fear?"

But God has put the body together, giving greater honor to the parts that lacked it, so that there should be no division in the body, but that its parts should have equal concern for each other. If one part suffers, every part suffers with it; if one part is honored, every part rejoices with it.

1 CORINTHIANS 12:24-26

WE COMPARE OURSELVES to others constantly, even (or, perhaps, especially) within the church. We feel there are certain giftings that draw the limelight, and this leaves us not always appreciating what God has placed in our hands. Rewind thousands of years and we see this is nothing new. Even within this chapter, it is baffling how many times Paul has to reiterate all of gifts come from the same God. Six times. It seems we all need to be reminded that God's playing field is a level one. Paul not only assures us all gifts have a part to play, but also that every single one will be honored.

Paul's analogy of a "body" isn't a foreign concept for first century readers. Roman culture used the word to define the nature of civic society. As with every society, there were honorable parts as well as dishonorable. In the Roman hierarchy, honor was only thrown around at the top. God, however, flips that arrangement by "giving greater honor to the part that lacked it." In God's economy, no one lacks honor. No person, gifting or contribution is to be looked down upon. How do we know for sure? God himself promises he will directly exalt his people in 1 Peter 5. He calls for it here and now. The threads of God's church are so tightly woven that when one suffers, the fibers pull at everyone. Likewise, when one operates their God-given gift, everyone enjoys it. This is the call for God's people.

Be it now or later, honor is guaranteed for those who love the Lord. That is a big deal, because it liberates you from spending a lifetime seeking it out. It shifts your priorities from being liked, appreciated, or esteemed to simply being faithful. Think about the church leaders of the fastest-growing movements in the world. You probably have a few names that spring to mind based on podcasts or social media. But those having the greatest impact do not have platforms. They are nobodies. Iran, for instance, has seen more conversions in the last 20 years than the last 13 centuries combined. The gifted leaders who undergird this persecuted movement will never be recognized, and they couldn't care less about it. I think that is the goal: not to intentionally avoid recognition, but to become indifferent to it. It is worth asking ourselves the following: *has a need to be celebrated distracted us from the call to be faithful?*

But because of his great love for us, God, who is rich in mercy, made us alive with Christ even when we were dead in transgressions—it is by grace you have been saved.

EPHESIANS 2:4-5

AS A PASTOR, ONE OF THE HARDEST things to convince the people of our city is that they are dead in their transgressions. In my city of Vancouver, people spend their mornings jogging the sea wall, practicing mindfulness at the beach, and then picking up a gluten-free croissant on the way to work. They breathe in the crisp ocean air as happy endorphins flood their brain, making them feel peaceful and alive. This passage, however, is a potent reminder that as we breathe deep of this world, our souls can lie lifeless and cold. French philosopher Pierre Telliard De Chardin states, "We are not human beings having a spiritual experience. We are spiritual beings having a human experience."[31] In reality, the truest part of us drags behind our best attempts to feel alive in this physical world.

Some people can dismiss the gnawing sense of emptiness, as if breathing in the ocean air will fill the cavity. For many, it's better than coming to terms with being spiritually dead. But the only way to be resuscitated back to life is through the sacrificial work of Jesus on the cross. Similar to David (Ps.51:5), Isaiah (Isa 6:5), or Peter (Luke 5:8), it takes an honest and courageous self-examination to realize your need for a Savior.

When we gaze upon the cross, we are left with two options. We might deny reality, excuse our sin, and shift the blame to make our condition more palatable; we make our failures fit within the range of mercy we can muster up for ourselves. Or we live in reality and recognize no one has the amount of mercy needed for us but God, because of his great love for us. His mercy is perfect and it is toward you. And although Jesus has brought us back to life, we still need to be continuously aware of the rich mercy we have received. When others gaze upon the cross, they may only see a revolutionist, an unfortunate rabbi or a rebel to Rome hung on the shameful seat of death. But when God's people gaze upon the cross, we are once again reminded of the ultimate mercy being poured out for us.

The night before Herod was to bring him to trial, Peter was sleeping between two soldiers, bound with two chains, and sentries stood guard at the entrance. Suddenly an angel of the Lord appeared and a light shone in the cell. He struck Peter on the side and woke him up. "Quick, get up!" he said, and the chains fell off Peter's wrists.

ACTS 12:6-7

IT'S NOT LOOKING GREAT for the church. Arrests are being made and key players like James are being put to death. And when things can't get much worse, Peter is thrown into prison and left waiting for his execution. The cards are stacked against this small movement of God's people. Maybe you have felt similar. You receive bad news about your health and, before you have a chance to make sense of it, a crippling financial challenge hits you out of left field. Life has a way of providing you with a rapid succession of trials that leave you distraught and questioning how God could possibly pull you out of this. Perhaps friends have tried to encourage you by saying something like, "God won't give you more than you can handle," which is loosely rooted in 1 Corinthians 10:13. Yet, life definitely throws us more than we can handle. When Moses freed a nation, Daniel survived a night with lions, or Joshua took down the fortified walls of Jericho, I don't think any of them thought this was in their wheelhouse. The key part of the Corinthians passage is that God is the one who provides a way of escape.

In Acts, Peter is asleep. You can imagine his thoughts before dozing off – perhaps thinking about martyrs who have gone before him or what will happen to those he leaves behind. He has likely already resigned himself to his fate – but not God. Peter wakes up to a boot in the side and loosened shackles. This is so outside of what he assumes possible that he thinks he is dreaming. When you are in your darkest hour, do you believe God can carve a path forward for you? It's possible he miraculously intervenes by breaking shackles, but it also might mean he simply provides you grace for each day to move forward through the chaotic torrent. Regardless of the path, it is one you look back upon and recognize you could have never traversed alone. God led you through the impossible. When you are in the thick of it, remember. Remember what God has already done for you. Jesus has set you free at a high cost, and he won't abandon you now. He has a way forward.

Half of the wood he burns in the fire;
over it he prepares his meal,
he roasts his meat and eats his fill.
He also warms himself and says,
"Ah! I am warm; I see the fire."
From the rest he makes a god, his idol;
he bows down to it and worships.
He prays to it and says,
"Save me! You are my god!"
They know nothing, they understand nothing;

ISAIAH 44:16-18

OF ALL THE BRILLIANT LITERARY devices used in Scripture, mockery has to be one of my favorites. Isaiah takes no issue with poking holes in all the neighborhood idolatries. At the end of the day, however, Isaiah is just an oracle. Yahweh is the real one calling the bluff at the table. Even with the most impressive raw materials to craft totems of worship, man's best efforts to fabricate what is holy and sacred fall miserably short. Only God determines what is holy. Here, he mocks man's foolish attempts to determine which chunk of wood is worthy of worship and which is simply firewood. It is easy to lean back and join in the mockery, but the desire to make what is common into what is holy resides in every human heart (Rom. 1:23)

There is something so enticing about making gods of things and people on this side of the veil. Our hearts are pulled to find cheap substitutes for the Holy One in what is common, tactile, measurable, and controllable. But the cost is great. To worship anything other than God is a dehumanizing experience. God intrinsically links the worshiper to the object being worshiped; knowing what becomes of his image bearers when tied to false Gods. As one author explains, "God hates the thing that has reduced humans to nothing."[33] This is why there is such a prominent focus on idolatry in the Old Testament. God wants his people to be truly human, and that only happens with him at the center.

We may not have idols, shrines, and totems scattered around the house, but they are ever-present in the fabric of western society. Where do you find happiness? Who gives you value? What provides comfort? How do you medicate your anger and anxiety? Many of us subtly trade out the Holy One for work, relationships, or substances. While we may admit to the idolatry in this, our pride comforts us that at least our idols are sophisticated. They are understandable substitutes. In reality, however, they are no more holy than a chunk of wood. God is infinitely greater than the most compelling idols this world has to offer. Take a moment to examine what your pride has concealed. What have you wrongly justified in your heart? Moreover, how is that dehumanizing you?

"A farmer went out to sow his seed. As he was scattering the seed, some fell along the path; it was trampled on, and the birds ate it up. Some fell on rocky ground, and when it came up, the plants withered because they had no moisture. Other seed fell among thorns, which grew up with it and choked the plants. Still other seed fell on good soil. It came up and yielded a crop, a hundred times more than was sown." When he said this, he called out, "Whoever has ears to hear, let them hear." "This is the meaning of the parable: The seed is the word of God. Those along the path are the ones who hear, and then the devil comes and takes away the word from their hearts, so that they may not believe and be saved. Those on the rocky ground are the ones who receive the word with joy when they hear it, but they have no root. They believe for a while, but in the time of testing they fall away. The seed that fell among thorns stands for those who hear, but as they go on their way they are choked by life's worries, riches and pleasures, and they do not mature. But the seed on good soil stands for those with a noble and good heart, who hear the word, retain it, and by persevering produce a crop.

LUKE 8:4-8, 11-15

JESUS NOTES IN THIS PARABLE four different responses to the gospel, which he later explains in detail. The third option is the one that haunts me. Here, we see a person who hasn't outrightly denied Jesus but rather put him on the back burner. It is a faith that slows to a crawl as pleasure and wealth assume a higher priority.

There is a disturbing lie that tends to surface in modern Christianity: that Jesus can be thrown in the mix with our other priorities. In a sense, many Christians are, unknowingly, functioning polytheists. They have found a way to worship money, pleasure, comfort, success, and Jesus without much internal conflict. This means an individual can go to church, sing songs, and give money, but what Jesus truly measures, is what the person falls short in — "maturity." Our misled hearts think they can house many Lords. There will come, however, an inevitable day when anything in our hearts valued more than Jesus will "choke" out our faith.

The passage is a candid, but kind, reminder to all of us. We cannot get distracted from the main task of maturing in our faith. The goal here is to bear fruit. The third plant in this parable provokes us to ask if we are seeing any progress in our faith, or if our hearts have instead been flooded with life's worries. Paul shares Jesus' urging to "continue to work out your salvation with fear and trembling" (Phil 2:12). Instead of reflecting upon the last year and wondering if we invested properly or traveled enough, we should be weighing if we have become more loving, generous, and compassionate people. Maturing in our faith doesn't always happen at the pace we would like; nevertheless, it should be the highest priority in our waking hours.

In your relationships with one another, have the same mindset as Christ Jesus: Who, being in very nature God, did not consider equality with God something to be used to his own advantage; rather, he made himself nothing by taking the very nature of a servant, being made in human likeness. And being found in appearance as a man, he humbled himself by becoming obedient to death — even death on a cross! Therefore God has highly exalted him and bestowed on him the name that is above every name, so that at the name of Jesus every knee should bow, in heaven and on earth and under the earth, and every tongue confess that Jesus Christ is Lord, to the glory of God the Father.

PHILIPPIANS 2:5-8

PHILIPPIANS 2 MAPS OUT Jesus' ministry as an inverted bell curve. Starting in a place of glory, Jesus looks down at the wild torrent humanity has conjured up and voluntarily sinks to its furthest depths: "death – even death on a cross." He descends to do cosmic work. He takes on human flesh, postures himself as a servant, and submits to an execution stripped of any human dignity. He does this to undo the curse of sin, defang death, and make a way for sinners to be restored to the Father. The bell curve then bends drastically upward in his resurrection, ascension, and exaltation by the Father. It's the beautiful drama of the unexpected work of God unfolding through his son.

We cannot overemphasize how drastic of a bell curve this is. Jesus is God, which means he is wholly other. John 1:14 does an extraordinary job illustrating this: "the word became flesh." Jesus takes an infinite step down into our finite world. No one in history has come remotely close to lowering themselves and giving up as much as Jesus does to be with his people. It is immeasurable.

Paul reminds us that if our allegiance is to Jesus, it shouldn't be a surprise that we are expected to follow the same trajectory. Knowing God promises to one day exalt and glorify his people provides a lot of freedom in this life to follow Jesus as far down as we can.[34] It is not a descent into self-pity and deprecation, but service and sacrifice driven by the love of Christ in you; Jesus is, after all, the one who took "the very nature of a servant". When climbers rappel down a mountainside, they are guided by anchors – anchors fixed by a previous, and usually more experienced, climber. In the same way, as we give our lives to love others – showing generosity to those who need it, being truthful when it hurts, or extending mercy wholeheartedly – we begin to see the fixed anchors Christ has set before us.

> If we confess our sins, he is faithful and just and will forgive us our sins and purify us from all unrighteousness. If we claim we have not sinned,we make him out to be a liar and his word is not in us.
>
> *1 JOHN 1:9-10*

AUGUSTINE STATES, "The confession of evil works is the first beginning of good works." Here is a historical practice that sits awkwardly in modern Christianity. For some, a saturated market of self-help and personal growth resources eliminates the felt need for it. For others, sin is understood as the cause of their trauma and pain – a transgression of which they are a victim, not a perpetrator. Regardless of how we think about our sin, acknowledging it, taking responsibility, and grieving its ramifications has become a lost art. This is tragic.

Confession is not a duty, but a gift – a gift that keeps you grounded in reality. The only other option is deception. If your actions are inconsistent with your beliefs, your brain fights back by either changing the belief to accommodate the action or vice versa. It's called cognitive dissonance. When behaviors are engrained, the brain has an easier time shaping the attitudes around it. Have you experienced that? To lessen the sting of guilt, we explain it away. We sympathize with our biological urges, excuse our actions with cultural norms, or defend harmful talk with claims of being authentic. At its worst, this causes us to stop striving toward certain spiritual disciplines because we dismiss them as nothing more than unattainable ideals. At its core, it is self-deception.

The other way to deal with guilt and shame is to confront it head-on: to recognize the dissonance as a failure on our part to live according to Jesus' standards. We choose to feel the weight of our decision (or lack thereof), and we bring it to Jesus instead of excusing it. Exposing our sin to the light can be painful, but when you make space for what is true, it is met with the faithful mercy of God. Confession does not deny, excuse, or diminish our sin, but rather confronts it in the company of a forgiving Savior. When we feel caught in cycles of sin with no way forward, self-deception can be a temporary antidote to the gnawing feelings of guilt and shame. Jesus has more for us. Jesus offers freedom for those who choose the hard, but truthful, road. This starts with confession, which is, Augustine reminds us, "the first beginning of good works."

Then God said, "Let us make mankind in our image, in our likeness, so that they may rule over the fish in the sea and the birds in the sky, over the livestock and all the wild animals, and over all the creatures that move along the ground." So God created mankind in his own image, in the image of God he created them; male and female he created them. God blessed them and said to them, "Be fruitful and increase in number; fill the earth and subdue it. Rule over the fish in the sea and the birds in the sky and over every living creature that moves on the ground." Then God said, "I give you every seed-bearing plant on the face of the whole earth and every tree that has fruit with seed in it. They will be yours for food."

GENESIS 1:26-29

WHAT EXACTLY ARE WE? In the creation story, God gives us a rundown of some key features that help answer this question. First, in verse 26, God shapes our identity as "image bearers." The word "image" (tselem) can be translated as shadow. It is as if, by walking so closely with God, we assume the role of God's representatives on earth. The remainder of the verse indicates this comes with a serious amount of authority over his creation. Not bad.

But before we feel too high and mighty, verse 29 sobers us up with a counterbalance that keeps us from flying too close to the sun.

God plants fruit trees in his garden for all his creatures – including us. We may be image bearers who will one day judge angels (1 Cor. 6:3), but so too are we creatures in God's order that eat, sleep, and breathe. As God formed Adam from the dust, we come to terms with the fact that we are from the earth and operate in harmony with every other living creature.

So, we find our answer sandwiched between these two identities. We are fearfully and wonderfully made image bearers set aside to represent God and steward the created world, yet we are deeply dependent on him for life, meaning, fulfillment, and our existence. This is a definition that can't be divorced from God. In short, we know ourselves only if we know God.

In a world with so many scattered and harmful definitions of self, this begins to anchor us in reality. On one side, we can find ourselves in the ditch of if it feels good, do it – a mentality wholly incompatible with those who are set apart to represent God. On the other side, the ditch that exhausts you by being all things to all people slams against your God-given creaturely limits. God anchors us in the middle as we are designed to be. The question is, when you look in the mirror, do you see a person slipping into one of these ditches?

Then some stood up and gave this false testimony against him: "We heard him say, 'I will destroy this temple made with human hands and in three days will build another, not made with hands.'" Yet even then their testimony did not agree. Then the high priest stood up before them and asked Jesus, "Are you not going to answer? What is this testimony that these men are bringing against you?" But Jesus remained silent and gave no answer.

MARK 14:57-61

HERE IS JESUS, BLAMELESS. The perfect judge over all things. Now, after a sleepless night of praying, he is dragged into a makeshift trial to be accused by twisted testimonies under the cover of night. Cowards, liars, and hypocrites are all driven by one unified goal of getting Jesus to the execution chair. This wasn't an unfamiliar place for Jesus. Throughout the gospel accounts, Jesus walks a minefield of false accusations. Whether for abandoning the law or rubbing shoulders with the devil, Jesus was continually put on trial for ridiculous claims. And every time Jesus eloquently counters with a single perfectly-placed answer – one that upholds the law while simultaneously rebuking the religious accusers and revealing his kingdom to his disciples. Every single time. So once again, with his life on the line more than ever, we expect a masterful rebuttal and get...silence. Why?

There is something more important than our need to defend ourselves: obedience to the Father. In this critical moment, Jesus reveals to all of humanity his unwavering allegiance to the Father's will. You won't find a more potent and raw image of self-denial in history than right here. This image should resonate in our hearts as we strive to follow the will of the Father – but, easier said than done. Honestly, we scarcely make room for God's input.

Here's the deal: if we feel obliged to give God a seat at the table only because he is a wise teacher who leads us to the good life, we will always weigh his counsel against ours. But he is more than that. He is the one who bought us for a price, liberating us from slavery and paying for our sins in full. He is our Lord, Master, and King. This demands a different type of relationship, one defined by radical trust and recognition of the Father as the only way to life. It is the sometimes painful practice of believing the Father is up to something grander, more beautiful, more pure and more impactful than what we may or may not ever see. Nevertheless, we are called to submit, and Jesus shows us how at this trial.

The areas of your life out of step with the Father might come to mind easily. Perhaps they don't. Take some time today to consider what part of you needs to be pulled into God's will.

Do not love the world or anything in the world. If anyone loves the world, love for the Father is not in them. For everything in the world—the lust of the flesh, the lust of the eyes, and the pride of life—comes not from the Father but from the world. The world and its desires pass away, but whoever does the will of God lives forever.

1 JOHN 2:15-17

I REMEMBER WATCHING 50 teams compete in a 670 km jungle terrain race called the Eco-Challenge. Racing alongside all the elite athletes was a 72-year-old veteran of the sport. Recently struck with Alzheimer's disease, he knew this was his last race. His son – capable of winning the race on his own – decided to run the race in tandem with his father. They weren't surprised to be at the back of the pack throughout the challenge; afterall, the once unstoppable athlete now needed help simply putting on his gloves and jacket. His back gave out at one point, and they ended up not even finishing the race. Regardless, it was this old man and his son who stole the show. Why? The human experience resonates with selfless love more than simply achieving greatness. The inspiration of watching a son give up his moment of glory to carry his father through one more race overshadowed any recognition of the great athletes competing at their highest levels.

Although sacrificial love inspires us, it is met with hostility by something lurking within – pride. Selfless acts of love are often blocked by ego and self-importance. When these are in the driver's seat, opportunities for meaningful relationships are left by the wayside; the impulse to relate to others gives way to the need to outshine them. We need community. Pride forces isolation. It makes no room for honesty, vulnerability, weakness, or humility, and these are defining features of authentic community. To be vulnerable and open yourself up to sacrificial love is what has the ability to bind us together in our shared humanity.

Here is the bigger problem: pride tends to have a reverberating effect into our relationship with God. Flannery O'Conner confesses, "Dear God, I cannot love Thee the way I want to. You are the slim crescent of a moon that I see and myself is the earth's shadow that keeps me from seeing all the moon . . . what I am afraid of, dear God, is that my self shadow will grow so large that it blocks the whole moon, and that I will judge myself by the shadow that is nothing. I do not know You God because I am in the way."[36] To be Christian is to actively put pride to death in our lives. This week, there might come a time when you should be last or go unrecognized so that others can be great and seen. Take a moment to prayerfully consider what that might look like for you.

Dear friends, let us love one another, for love comes from God. Everyone who loves has been born of God and knows God. Whoever does not love does not know God, because God is love.

1 JOHN 4:7-8

GOD IS LOVE. Every neighbor's yard raked, love letter written, father-son moment experienced, or breakfast in bed delivered: they are all reverberations of God's love towards His creation. There is no other source of love in the cosmos; it all comes from Him. Yet, for many, the resonance of this love through people isn't always felt. It's sparse and irregular. One author describes it as a couple of beautiful notes coincidently strung together in an otherwise horrid song.[37] Those of us "born of God" have ears tuned by God to hear a masterpiece played for eternity: His everlasting love. As we experience it, it vibrates through our chest cavity and changes us. We become attuned to listening for it in everyday places. We learn its melody and begin harmonizing along. John captures this earlier in his letter: "See what great love the Father has lavished on us, that we should be called children of God" (3:1). We become people marked by this love.

If those who love are born of God, we probably expect those who don't love to be transgressors. Yet, John simply attributes their lack of love to not knowing God. They haven't really heard the song for which they are made.

In an annual Nepalese tradition, thousands of young people visit a sacred statue called Swet Bhairav. For this short window of time, rice wine drips out of the statue's mouth. And people are frantic for it. They climb over each other, clawing their way forward to get just a drop of this wine on their tongues. They believe the wine connects them to the transcendent, to Shiva. It's a great example of what we already know to be true: a new generation desperately wants something more than what the world has to offer. One study shows almost 40% of the next generation is on a quest for spiritual truth.[38] They have heard the broken record playing over and over, and they want something more.

This changes how we think about the people we encounter. Our call isn't to grasp for the moral high ground or take sides in a culture war. It is about sharing God's love for us and hoping others hear a bit of the song too. At the end of the day, the only reason we can love is because we know the one who loved us first.

The fire on the altar must be kept burning; it must not go out. Every morning the priest is to add firewood and arrange the burnt offering on the fire and burn the fat of the fellowship offerings on it.

LEVITICUS 6:12

THERE WAS A GOD-ORDAINED expectation for priests to ensure the altar fire kept burning. With the law being handed to Moses and the Tabernacle being prepared, these were the early days of establishing a covenantal framework for God's people. There wasn't a lot of wiggle room to get it wrong. The priests had to keep the fire burning.

How often do you read your Bible? It's not a comfortable question, as many of us have a strange relationship with the book. I get it: the Bible is ancient. The cultural gap is vast and, at times, the relevancy takes work to find. On top of that, we are generally wary about anything that comes with the expectation of a regimented routine. It feels religious and disingenuous within the fluid and authentic journey of faith. It is, however, is the word of life (Phil 2:16). What we feel about it doesn't change that.

How do we get past the obstacles that prevent us from enjoying the word of life? Discipline. James K Smith writes, "The orientation of the heart happens from the bottom up, through the formation of our habits of desire. Learning to love God takes practice."[39] Bringing about change in your heart starts with forming the right habits.

When I was a teenager, I hated the taste of coffee; however, I drank it because it was the cool adult thing to do. Now, it is the most enjoyable drink of my day. What started out as an unsatisfying practice became, over time, a joy. Sometimes discipline has to lead the way for affection to follow, not the other way around.

I am sure there were mornings when the priests didn't feel like throwing wood on the fire. Yet, they knew it was an essential part of how the covenantal people lived in relation to God. They didn't let their tired bodies or disinterested minds lead the charge, but rather their conviction to be connected to life. I wonder if we see it that way. Dragging ourselves out of bed to read isn't just to find some advice or encouragement for the day, but to throw another log on the fire that sustains our lives.

At this the Jews there began to grumble about him because he said, "I am the bread that came down from heaven." They said, "Is this not Jesus, the son of Joseph, whose father and mother we know? How can he now say, 'I came down from heaven'?"

JOHN 6:41-42

RELEVANT MAGAZINE HAS PEGGED our current moment as the 'Age of Deconstructionism'.[40] A multitude of factors play into this growing problem, but the heart of it resides in this passage. Here we have a group of people struggling to commit anything more to Jesus. Their biggest hang-up is familiarity. They were introduced to him not when he was miraculously healing lepers, but when he was playing with the neighbor's kids. They saw the Son of God in the mundane and common, not the extravagant and supernatural. And the claim that heaven is his primary residence is too big of a leap for those who grew up in his neighborhood. The Jesus they know and the one being presented cannot co-exist in their heads.

Many of us have had a similar divergence. We are introduced to a spectacular Jesus; then, through our experiences with the church, spiritual leaders, and other professing christians, our once-fervent faith begins to deflate. We have seen enough, and the math doesn't add up. Doubts about scripture start gnawing at our minds and the facade of Christian holiness starts gnawing at our soul. Some of us take our faith all the way to ground-zero and ask the most fundamental question: is Jesus even that spectacular?

Deconstructionism has become a signpost that Christianity is something to grow out of. However, what many describe as a dead end is actually a fork in the road. Jesus stands at the intersection and invites all those who are no longer satisfied with Sunday school answers into a richer and more robust faith (1 Corinthians 3:2). Read the rest of the chapter: it is mostly Jesus drawing the crowd into a more holistic and exhaustive understanding of what he is up to. Today, he creates the same opportunities for the doubting heart to rediscover him in a way that holds up against the complexities, challenges, inconsistencies, and chaos of life.

You may not be questioning the existence of God, but we have all hit a couple potholes along the journey that call us to re-examine what exactly we believe about God. In the very beginning of Psalms the author likens us to trees near running water (Psalms 1:3). As we hit these potholes, the call is to push our roots deeper into the soil. We must aspire to have a theology that isn't made up of shallow rootlets, but rather ones that push past the hard soils and rocks for sustenance. There's no way to soft pitch this: it involves work. To press deeper into the soil demands not only a diligent mind, but a hungry heart that regularly feeds on "the bread that came down from heaven".

Yes, my soul, find rest in God;
my hope comes from him.
Truly he is my rock and my salvation;
he is my fortress, I will not be shaken.
My salvation and my honor depend on God;
he is my mighty rock, my refuge.
Trust in him at all times, you people;
pour out your hearts to him,
for God is our refuge.

PSALMS 62:5-8

IF YOU COMPARE TRANSLATIONS, you will notice that the word "rest" (dāmam) in the first verse is replaced with "silence" in a handful of versions. In the Hebrew language, there is some serious overlap between the two. But that is not how we have been pitched rest in today's world. For us, rest simply means to shift gears from work-related activities to pleasurable activities. To slow down entirely seems foreign to our bodies. The idea of not only letting up the pace, but entering into silence is a literal nightmare for most. However, to have a meaningful relationship with God, you have to stop, be quiet, and listen. The three persons of the Triune God have been conversing since eternity past, and because of Christ's work, by the Spirit, you get to be ushered into the conversation. It's probably wise to not walk in yapping.

Bringing silence to your prayer life is like walking your commute to work instead of driving. You become much more attentive to things you've driven by daily. Whether it be by noticing a newly found bakery, a hidden walking path, or a housing development, your commute becomes more expansive at a slower pace. When the Psalmist slows down, his relationship with God becomes expansive. When you are silent, you can't fill the air with talk: you must sit and experience who God is. You are drawn into His expansive grandness. Therefore it is only fitting for the Psalmist to conclude from a place of rest that God is the ultimate refuge for him. Spending time and waiting on God does something to you. You become grounded in his salvation.

The Psalmist declares he will not be shaken. Isn't that what we all want? To not so easily be thrown around by the waves of life? Silence isn't a breathing exercise for regulating emotions – it is a space for you to once again find your footing in the work of Christ. So do what is unnatural for you until it becomes natural: slow down and be silent. It's not easy, but God calls all of us to "be still, and know that [he is] God" (Ps. 46:10).

> You are the light of the world. A town built on a hill cannot be hidden. Neither do people light a lamp and put it under a bowl. Instead they put it on its stand, and it gives light to everyone in the house. In the same way, let your light shine before others, that they may see your good deeds and glorify your Father in heaven.
>
> *MATTHEW 5:14-16*

WHEN WE CONSIDER HOW to be involved in our local church, we tend to choose the aspects that directly benefit us. There's nothing wrong with this; afterall, we need to make space for our own spiritual growth. But that's only part of the grand vision of discipleship. Think about Jesus' mandate for our lives. What does a light gain from lighting up a home? Nothing. What does a home gain from a light illuminating it? Everything. This offers a different perspective on how we engage with our local church. For example, when weighing whether or not to join a small group, the determining factor shouldn't be whether or not you already have healthy friendships, but rather if there are people in your church who might need a friend in you.

Our faith naturally becomes insular if we are not paying attention. The last thing I want is to have a life lived under a bowl. However, it is imperative we also understand that being a light means more than giving additional time to volunteerism. In the Gospel of John, Jesus identifies himself as light in one of his seven "I am" statements. Jesus himself is the light, not us. John Calvin explains, "Man reflects, like a mirror, the wisdom, righteousness, and goodness of God." The key difference between being "under a bowl" or being placed "on a stand" is positioning: on a stand, our whole life is positioned toward Jesus. There is nothing in ourselves that illuminates the darkness. But if we shift our gaze towards Jesus, like a mirror, we begin to reflect the beauty, goodness, and love of Jesus to others.

So yes, be a light that is focused outwardly towards your church, friends, strangers, and enemies, but realize that to have any meaningful impact, you must first orient yourself toward the "light of the world." In the Old Testament, Moses came down Mount Sinai with a shining face after spending days in God's presence. It was so radiant the people gave him a veil to cover it up. It wasn't his leadership, strategy, or even faithfulness that earned him that light. Moses lit up because he conversed with the light of the world. Our faces might not shimmer at work after listening to a devotion on the commute, but the principal remains. When you make time to truly gaze upon one whose face is like the sun shining in all its brilliance (Rev. 1:16), you find yourself wanting to reflect it wherever you can.

In the beginning God created the heavens and the earth. Now the earth was formless and empty, darkness was over the surface of the deep, and the Spirit of God was hovering over the waters.

GENESIS 1:1-2

THE DOCTRINE OF THE TRINITY isn't the easiest to grasp. What was articulated as early as the 2nd century by Tertullian, Clement of Alexandria, and Origen and then formally established as doctrine in the 4th century, still leaves us scratching our heads a bit. How does it all work and does it have any effect on my day to day life? There is a gem in the creation narrative that, if we are to catch a glimpse of it, shows us the outlandish love of the Triune God.

Think about it. Why did God create the universe in the first place? Out of boredom or loneliness? If he is self-sufficient, why bother creating anything outside himself? Understanding his motivation is critical to understanding his nature. The Triune God is uniquely positioned to be a God who is loving for eternity's past. Michael Reeves brilliantly identifies the challenges with a "solidarity God," like Allah, being described as "The Loving" without having anyone or anything to love before creation. Even more problematic, Allah is then dependent on creation to be who he is – a loving God.[42] Yet, the biblical narrative tells us The Father, Son and Spirit "were happy in themselves, and enjoyed one another before the world was."[43] There has always existed a perfect outpouring of love across the three persons of the Great I AM.

Reeves describes God as a fountain. Life and love flow out of him. He must pour forth. It is in his nature. Therefore, creation is an overflow of the outpouring of love between the Triune God. Karl Barth states it this way, "He does not wish to be without hearing or echo, that is, without the ears and voices of the creature. The eternal fellowship between Father and Son, or between God and His Word, thus finds a correspondence in the very different but not dissimilar fellowship between God and His creature."[44] The universe exists because God is love. The entire foundation of our existence is constructed by his love.

This changes how you see your place in the universe: you are a product of God's overflowing love. You are not an accident or a mistake, but intentionally-designed with the purpose to love and receive love. In the words of Barth, God desires for his creatures to have ears to hear his love and voices to respond back. It is a love that binds us in fellowship with our Triune God. Today, dare to believe in his love for you not because of what you deserve, but because of His amazing love for you regardless.

Then Jesus declared, "I am the bread of life. Whoever comes to me will never go hungry, and whoever believes in me will never be thirsty.

JOHN 6:35

JESUS MAKES SEVEN "I AM" STATEMENTS in the Gospel of John; this one comes on the heels of his miraculous act of feeding five thousand people. A group of skeptics, however, still have some conditions before buying into Jesus' movement. Big fans of Moses' miracles, they want to see Jesus similarly create manna from heaven. The bread Jesus miraculously multiplied literally still sits comfortably in their bellies! However, instead of reminding them of what they just experienced, he seizes the opportunity to make a point. Working with their understanding of the Moses story, he introduces them to a different bread that also comes down from heaven, but gives life to the world: himself.

When we partake in communion, the focus is often on Jesus' broken body and the cost of sin on the cross. As important as it is to see communion as a symbol of death, it is also a symbol of life. Later in the chapter, Jesus is a bit more direct: "Very truly I tell you, unless you eat the flesh of the Son of Man and drink his blood, you have no life in you" (John 6:53). We regularly partake of the bread and wine to remember the sacrifice made by Jesus, but also the abundant life found in Him. As the Hebrews needed manna to continue their desperate journey through the desert, we need Jesus as our manna to continue through the desperate journey of life. He is nourishment for our soul, joy for our pain, and strength to our faith. The Bread of Life is our sustenance.

This single verse is a gold mine of promise. What makes it especially rich are the words “whoever comes.” Jesus’ life is available to anyone in need of nourishing life. No matter what you have done or from where you come, the invitation is the same. If your soul feels depleted, if your heart feels inadequate, or if your mind feels overwhelmed, the call is to be nourished by the Bread of Life.

You are worthy, our Lord and God,
to receive glory and honor and power,
for you created all things,
and by your will, they were created
and have their being.

REVELATION 4:11

THERE IS A GOOD CHANCE you are reading this with your phone next to you on the couch, and we both know it's only a matter of time before the screen lights up. It could be as simple as an email notification, but it's still enough to pull your attention in. No shame, I'm there a lot of days. Boredom and distraction become annoying company in our pursuit to meet with God. We know God is worthy to "receive glory and honor and power," but there are plenty of mornings he doesn't receive that from me. Turning our phones off and finding a quiet space or an unhurried calendar all help combat the issue, but the reality is boredom finds its origin in our hearts. How do we solve this?

It never hurts to step back and examine the structure of your prayer life. Tim Keller breaks down prayer into three categories. First, there are outward prayers. These are prayers for our world and the people in our lives. Second, there are inward prayers. These are times of contemplation and confession, drawing attention to our intimate dialogue with God. Lastly, there are upward prayers. These are prayers of thanksgiving, awe, and praise. All three categories of prayer don't have to be perfectly balanced, but I do find the first two tend to outweigh the last. Prayers that primarily focus on my needs, my condition, and my sin build a prayer life that is fairly repetitive, simple, and boring because it is all about me.

The Lord's Prayer tells us to ask for our daily bread – that's good! But the order of how Jesus teaches us to pray is interesting. In Matthew 6:9, Jesus opens with, "Our Father in heaven, hallowed be your name." He starts with upward prayer, and that is important. When our prayers begin by circling around God and who he is, we are reminded of with whom we are conversing. What makes him worthy begins to flood our minds and frame the remaining conversation. Henri Nouwen states, "Praise and adoration are the necessary preconditions for the proper formulation and motivation of all the other kinds of prayer."[46] So, how do we dig out boredom and distraction from our hearts? How do we properly give God the glory and honor he deserves? Consider starting your devotions by stating the obvious. Pray upward to remind yourself that you are on holy ground.

The teachers of the law and the Pharisees brought in a woman caught in adultery. They made her stand before the group and said to Jesus, "Teacher, this woman was caught in the act of adultery. In the Law Moses commanded us to stone such women. Now what do you say?" They were using this question as a trap, in order to have a basis for accusing him. But Jesus bent down and started to write on the ground with his finger. When they kept on questioning him, he straightened up and said to them, "Let any one of you who is without sin be the first to throw a stone at her."

JOHN 8:3-7

THE COST OF DISCIPLESHIP isn't something we can get around. Following Jesus puts a real demand on our life. Refusing to conform to the pattern of this world (Romans 12:2) can involve some serious heavy lifting, the bulk of this strain coming from the notion of dying to ourselves (Gal. 2:20) – not an easy endeavor. Wrestling our life into submission to Jesus and giving him permission to chart our course doesn't come naturally to us. To be a disciple is to live in that tension continually. Or is it?

The Pharisees believed they had found a route to God that didn't demand much dying at all. In fact, their religious accolades tended to feed their flesh instead of helping them wrestle it to death. They had found a safe haven in religion – what they viewed as the correct theology fed their sense of self-righteousness and status in their culture. So, they engaged with Jesus on their playing field and challenged him to a theological debate. Jesus didn't play ball. After being bated over and over, Jesus topples their facade of holiness in one sweeping statement: "Let any one of you who is without sin be the first to throw a stone at her." He cuts right to the core of each accuser. The place where real discipleship takes place – the soul.

Following Jesus isn't easy. There are tempting off-ramps available, ones we can take while deceiving ourselves into thinking we are still on course. You can simplify discipleship into believing a specific worldview, subscribing to a set of ethics, voting for a particular party, or accepting a certain theological tradition, but to do so is to miss Jesus. Jesus doesn't just want your viewpoints – he wants all of you. And what you will find as you struggle to wholly submit yourself to him is that there is a sweetness in the struggle. It is not submission for submission's sake, but one that leads us to freedom, healing, and purpose.

Do an inventory with God. While you may want to keep things surface-level, is Jesus wanting to go deeper with you today?

For I was hungry and you gave me something to eat, I was thirsty and you gave me something to drink, I was a stranger and you invited me in, I needed clothes and you clothed me, I was sick and you looked after me, I was in prison and you came to visit me.

MATTHEW 25:35-36

THERE ARE SO MANY WAYS to serve Jesus. Often, we see these opportunities on a Sunday: teaching bible stories to children, leading the pre-service prayer meeting, or playing the keyboard for the worship team. Why these examples come to mind first is understandable. Our impulse is to evaluate an endeavour's success by its scale of impact, and successful service to Jesus is no exception. Jesus, however, has different markers.

Matthew 25:35-36 shines a spotlight on areas of need we sometimes forget. The poor, the needy, the foreigner, and the helpless in obscure and forgotten places all seem to have Jesus' attention. Jesus has an affinity with the poor, as the God of the universe literally stepped into poverty. He was born in a feeding trough, raised in a humble town, and did ministry with no possessions or residence (Matt.8:20). In fact, what became a massive deterrent for a handful of would-be disciples was an unwillingness to live at the same standard of means as Jesus. Jesus readily chose to connect himself to the poor.

When we serve the poor or the marginalized, there may not be the clear return on investment for which we all secretly hope. It may be hard to see how the act contributes to the kingdom of God. Jesus, however, makes the intrinsic connection clear: when you serve the poor, it is as if you serve Jesus himself. You patiently made time to listen to Jesus at the homeless shelter. You faithfully provided groceries for him in his home. Proverbs 19:17 tells us that if we give to the poor, we are lending to God. I don't know of a more vivid image of service relating directly to God in Scripture.

This, of course, doesn't render your efforts as a church usher void; it simply provides us with a more holistic understanding of serving Jesus. The call for every disciple is to not only serve the affluent, the socially-adept, the familiar, or the well-networked, but image bearers of God who have absolutely nothing to offer in return. Because that's what Jesus did for us.

And I saw a beast rising out of the sea, with ten horns and seven heads, with ten diadems on its horns and blasphemous names on its heads. And the beast that I saw was like a leopard; its feet were like a bear's, and its mouth was like a lion's mouth. And to it the dragon gave his power and his throne and great authority.

REVELATION 13:1-3

HERE IS A PASSAGE THAT probably didn't make your memory verse list as a kid. Its bizarre apocalyptic language can throw us for a loop. Basically, Jesus is allowing John to have a peek behind the scenes of history unfolding. It isn't strictly a snapshot of Jesus' return. Jonathan Pageau likens it to kneading dough: the end product is already present in the ingredients of the dough, you just can't see it yet. Those ingredients are primarily the death, resurrection, and ascension of Jesus. The book of Revelation, therefore, isn't just about pinpointing future events, but also revealing what already is in its fullness: namely, the beast.

What's the deal with the beast? Daniel experiences a similar vision in the Old Testament. He sees animal characters who also come out of the sea (Daniel 7:3). Those four creatures each represent political power antithetical to God's kingdom. Revelation combines them into a single physical representation of an evil that has lurked throughout history: empires that oppose God's work. Pharaoh, Nero, Galerius, Hitler, Stalin, and Mao all drank deep of the dragon's influence and aspired to deify their position. Many Christians have been trampled under the beastly claws of these leaders.

Here's what is truly terrifying: the same beastly compulsion lies deep in the undisturbed waters of our hearts. Craig Keener asserts, "What should frighten us even more is that the same spirit of the self-deifying empire remains in every human heart that seeks to make itself the center of life while burying thoughts of its own mortality." It may not involve the same level of savagery, but the desire to be like God is a common thread that connects us all the way back to Adam holding a half-eaten fruit in the garden.

Life's pressures have a way of pushing to the surface selfish and untamed actions that seem unusual to us. We use dissociative language like, "That's very unlike me" or "I wasn't acting like myself." However, what's coming to the top might be our truest self. Our job as disciples is not to deflect, but rather embrace the reality that we still have work to do. We recognize that, like Pharaoh and Nero, there is something beastly at work in our hearts. Fortunately, God is in it with us. He is more than willing to overpower the beast, even at the deepest undisturbed layers of our soul. So don't try and wrestle the beast down on your own; you'll fail. Instead, be quiet, examine yourself, be honest, pray, and invite God into the battle.

To him who is able to keep you from stumbling and to present you before his glorious presence without fault and with great joy— to the only God our Savior be glory, majesty, power and authority, through Jesus Christ our Lord, before all ages, now and forevermore! Amen.

JUDE 24-25

THE ONLY GOD AND SAVIOR: this is Jesus. Lately, this idea has been a little lost in the weeds. There has been an interesting current in the preaching of Jesus' gospel primarily portrayed as the renewal of all things. It is what Matt Chandler calls the "gospel in the sky."[50] The cross is a cosmic catalyst to usher in his new kingdom. The way of Jesus leads to wholeness and restoration. This is true not only for ourselves, with a proper sense of work, meaning, relationships, and self-worth, but also in our communities concerning injustice and reconciliation. The gospel has implications for all of creation. Receiving it means receiving his kingdom and partaking in his overarching redemptive mission here and now.

There is also another vantage point from which to understand the gospel – what Chandler calls the "gospel on the ground." Because of the gospel, Jesus will receive you before his glorious presence without fault. Not only is the gospel about cosmic restoration, but personal redemption. Christ's death, resurrection, and ascension are the inauguration of all things new, which includes the hostile takeover of your soul from the kingdom of darkness to his kingdom. You were dead in your sins without hope, but because of Christ's atoning sacrifice on the cross, you have salvation into eternal life. That message matters. If you were to go back in time to 1944 and you had the opportunity to speak to dozens of Allied soldiers the night before they stormed the beaches of Normandy, what would you say? You have the attention of men who have become acutely aware that they are probably not going home. What hope can you provide them? It can't be a message of meaning, flourishing, or wholeness, since the veil of death becomes thin. It must be a message of grace, forgiveness, and salvation so they understand when they fall through that veil, they will enter God's glorious presence without fault.

Take a moment to go back to your roots. Remember with gratitude exactly from what Jesus saved you. Think about your current situation, and humbly reflect on what he is presently saving you from. Look to the future. Believe with hope and faith that one day he will save you. He is our Savior who has, is, and will save us.

To God's holy people in Colossae, the faithful brothers and sisters in Christ: Grace and peace to you from God our Father.

COLOSSIANS 1:2

HOW DOES SCRIPTURE DEFINE YOU? Your mind might take you to a word like "sinner." Seems on brand with your life. The word is used 32 times in the New Testament alone. We are sinners saved by grace, right? Kind of.

Guess how many times the word "sinner" is used in the present tense for a believer? Zero. Everytime that word is used, Paul is referring to a non-believer or the past life of a believer. He actually provides a much more flattering name for us: "God's holy people." Other versions translate the name as "saints" – 60 times in the New Testament, to be precise. Does that mean we never sin? No. Does that mean we don't have to confess our sins to one another? Not at all. It means God has provided us with a different identity paved by the blood of the Son and sealed by His Spirit. So it's rock solid. A saint resides at the core of every believer. This matters because how we understand ourselves drives everything we do. We all have defining memories of both horrific and beautiful words that settled into our subconscious understanding of self. When you look in the mirror and all you see is a reckless sinner, it's hard to envision the power of the cross enabling you to holiness; in some ways, it makes it easier for you to take advantage of your girlfriend's body, gossip about a family member, or bury yourself in work. You may not like these characteristics of yourself, but at least they are consistent with how you understand your makeup.

Now, if you were to once again return to God's portrait of your life, to remember what he has claimed to be true of you, how would you live today? For some of you that might take some serious faith as you feel the cards are stacked against you, but it is no less true. You are a saint because of Jesus. Nothing else. So, step into today with Philippians 3:13-14 at the forefront of your mind: "I do not consider myself yet to have taken hold of it. But one thing I do: Forgetting what is behind and straining toward what is ahead, I press on toward the goal to win the prize for which God has called me heavenward in Christ Jesus."

I have been crucified with Christ and I no longer live, but Christ lives in me. The life I now live in the body, I live by faith in the Son of God,who loved me and gave himself for me.

GALATIANS 2:20

IN CHRIST. Arguably, there is no greater claim in all of Scripture. Christian, saint, disciple, believer, or elect all pale in comparison to Paul's favorite nickname for the people of God: "in Christ." In this passage, you see a synergy between two realities. Firstly, Paul recognizes his old life has been crucified with Jesus and by faith, his life is now found in the Son of God. Secondly, and simultaneously, Paul claims because of Jesus' death on his behalf, Christ lives in him. He is in Christ, and Christ is in him; this is the union of Christ, and it matters.

There is a stubborn lie – like black mold in the corner of the shower – that keeps making its way back into our lives: the lie that we need to work for our righteousness. But being "in Christ" means Jesus is our representative. Much like David representing the Israelites in the duel against Goliath, or our team winning a gold medal in the Olympics, you have this real sense that his win is your win. But what Jesus has accomplished is more than a sense. In his definitive victory on the cross, Jesus makes a spectacle of all principalities, authorities, and death itself (Col 2:15). We get to stand on the podium with him and receive a gold medal too. His victory over death becomes ours as people hidden in Him (Col. 3:3). We all know there are days where this doesn't feel true. Our prayer life wanes, our pride takes over, the office gossip gets the best of us, or we simply lose sight of God's mission. In those moments, we must return to the gospel and remember he did all the heavy lifting. We are completely justified before the Father because we "have been crucified with Christ."

Not only do we abide in Him, but, as Paul states, "Christ lives in me." The work of the cross not only claims we are righteous, but empowers us to pursue a life of righteousness. Jesus settles into our lives, but isn't always the most accommodating house guest; he tends to move a lot of furniture around in our soul. Unapologetically, his agenda is to give us a new heart (Ezek. 36:26), a new mind (1 Cor. 2:16), and a new self (2 Cor. 5:16). That usually involves some serious renovations. We don't only hide in Christ, we begin to look like Him. Salvation isn't only claimed, but applied. It is the marriage of justification and sanctification in the union of Christ. You are justified so you can be with God, and you are sanctified because you have been with God.

NOTES

1. Williams, D. J. (2011). Acts: Understanding the Bible commentary. InterVarsity Press.

2. Insights from Darrell Johnson at Pastoral Retreat

3. Kierkegaard, S. 239 (2002). Provocations: Spiritual writings of Kierkegaard (C. E. Moore, Ed.). Plough Publishing House

4. Verse one is debated, but Hans-Joachim Kraus makes a compelling argument in The Book of Psalms: Volume II, Psalms 73–150, 852 NCB (Grand Rapids: Eerdmans, 1981)

5. Smith, J. K. A. 100 (2016). You Are What You Love: The Spiritual Power of Habit. Brazos Press

6. Saint Augustine, Confessions, trans. Henry Chadwick (Oxford: Oxford University Press, 1991), 3.

7. Young, W. P. (2007). The shack. Windblown Media.

8. Jesus actually offers her living water, which is a symbol for the Holy Spirit. John confirms this in John 7.

9. Sprinkle, P. (Host). (2024, Jul 15) Does The Church Have a Crisis of Biblical Illiteracy, Jen Wilkin. In Theology in the Raw *[https://theologyintheraw.com/podcast/does-the-church-have-a-crisis-of-biblical-illiteracy-jen-wilkin/]*

10. Packer, J. I. 73 (1973). Knowing God. InterVarsity Press

11. Packer, J. I. 133

12. In The Da Vinci Code, Dan Brown makes the claim that Jesus was married to Mary

13. Murray, J. (1955). Redemption accomplished and applied. Eerdmans

14. Swoboda, A. J. (2018). Subversive Sabbath: The surprising power of rest in a nonstop world. Brazos Press

15. Keller, T. (2007, February 25). John 13 [Audio recording]. Gospel in Life. https://www.gospelinlife.com/john-13

16. Johnson, J. 56 (2010). Abundant simplicity: Discovering the unhurried rhythms of grace. IVP Books.

17. Tozer, A. W. 75 (1982). The pursuit of God. Christian Publications. (Original work published 1948)

18. Kensrue, D. (2012). All glory be to Christ [Song]. On The Water & the Blood. Mars Hill Music

19. To be clear, the author isn't attributing sexual temptation to any specific gender, but has personified sexual temptation as a figurative unfaithful wife.

20. James 3:13-18

21. Goggin, J., & Strobel, K. (2017). The Way of The Dragon or The Way of The Lamb: Searching for Jesus' Path of Power in a Church That Has Abandoned It. Thomas Nelson.

22. Willard, D. 198 (2006). The Great Omission: Reclaiming Jesus' Essential Teachings on Discipleship. HarperOne.

23. Dearman, A. J. 322 (2002). Lamentations. In T. Muck (Ed.), The NIV application commentary. Zondervan.

24. Desmond Tutu: A Spiritual Biography, directed by Barbara Rick (New York: Out of The Blue Films, 2004).

25. Crowe, J. 89 (2021). Open the Bible. Moody Publishers

26. The ESV Bible (Crossway, 2001)

27. Keller, T. 21 (2014). Prayer: Experiencing awe and intimacy with God. Penguin Books

28. Lewis, C. S. 81, (1961). A grief observed. HarperOne.

29. Carey Nieuwhof (2024, Jan 25) John Ortberg Breaks Down the Divide Between Leadership and Spiritual Formation [https://www.youtube.com/watch?v=wdb_pNAs380]

30. Wright, S. (2021, June 22). The damnation of Venice: Locals are being systematically driven out by officials who are selling off sites for tourism.

31. Nouwen, H. J. M. 44 (1974). Out of solitude: Three Meditations on the Christian Life. Darton, Longman & Todd.

32. Pierre Teilhard de Chardin, 288. The Phenomenon of Man, trans. Bernard Wall (New York: Harper & Row, 1959)

33. Oswalt, J. N. 291 (2003). NIV application commentary: Isaiah. Zondervan.

34. Romans 8:30, James 4:10 and 1 Corinthians 12:23

35. Augustine. 370 (1990). Expositions of the Psalms (Enarrationes in Psalmos) (M. Boulding, Trans.). New City Press. (Original work published ca. 400)

36. O'Connor, F. (2013). A prayer journal. Farrar, Straus and Giroux. (Original work published 1957)

37. Sermon from Jonathan Edwards

38. Barna Group. (2019). The connected generation: How Christian leaders around the world can address the beliefs, behaviors, and experiences of millennials and gen z. Barna Group

39. Smith, J. K. A. 100 (2016). You Are What You Love: The Spiritual Power of Habit. Brazos Press

40. Schaeffer, J. (2024, August 23). The age of deconstruction and the future of the church. Relevant Magazine. https://relevantmagazine.com

41. Calvin, J. (1847). Commentary on Genesis (King J., Trans.). Calvin Translation Society. (Original work published 1554)

42. Reeves, M. (2012). Delighting in the Trinity: An introduction to the Christian faith. IVP Academic.

43. Sibbes, R. 195 (1862). The Successful Seeker. In A. B. Grosart (Ed.), The works of Richard Sibbes (Vol. 7, pp. 183–266). James Nichol.

44. Karl Barth, 48 (1959) Dogmatics in Outline, trans. G. T. Thompson. London: SCM Press

45. Keller, T. 189 (2014). Prayer: Experiencing awe and intimacy with God. Penguin Books

46. Nouwen, H. J. M. 30 (1976). The Genesee diary: Report from a Trappist monastery. Doubleday.

47. Jonathan Pageau, interview by Lex Fridman, Lex Fridman Podcast, episode #370, January 2023, accessed. https://lexfridman.com/jonathan-pageau-370/.

48. Keener, C. S. 118 (2000). Revelation (NIV Application Commentary). Zondervan

49. Chandler, M. 56 (2012). The Explicit Gospel. Crossway

50. Chandler, 40.

Made in the USA
Monee, IL
01 December 2024

66f9817e-4624-4c76-b6d2-a0448e6cc29bR01